FOLK ART APPLIQUE QUILTS

FOLK ART APPLIQUE QUILTS

Step by step instructions for 14 original quilts combining appliqué and piece-work
with occasional handpainted detail

DAWN FITZPATRICK

MEREHURST

LONDON

Acknowledgements

Special thanks to
Justin Fitzpatrick, Diana Cross, Mark Tuckey,
Elizabeth Brenchley and Susan Chenery

Designed by P.A.G.E. Pty Ltd
Illustrations by Peter Calvitto
Photography by Craig Cumming

Published 1990 by Merehurst Limited
Ferry House, 51/57 Lacy Road, Putney, London, SW15 1PR

By arrangement with Allen & Unwin Australia Pty Ltd

© Dawn Fitzpatrick 1990

ISBN 1–85391–170–4

Set in Palatino by P.A.G.E Pty Ltd, Carlton, 3053, Victoria

Printed in Singapore by Toppan

CONTENTS

INTRODUCTION

The clear and simple images that the early folk artists used to enrich their Spartan lives were created from scraps of iron, wood or paint left over from every-day use.

In today's jaded society this fact alone captures our imagination and these original icons of Folk Art frugality now adorn museums and the homes of the wealthy, while the less fortunate romantics buy mass-produced reproductions.

The aim of this book is to create a revival of this endearing custom of recording contemporary life for the comfort and delight of our families, but at the same time, speed up the process to keep pace with our rapid lifestyle.

During my convent school-days in the early thirties, we were taught hand sewing because a true lady would never contemplate using a sewing machine. Our first assignment was to make our school bloomers from navy Fuji silk, with French seams. We then progressed to making a petticoat, and finally the most exciting garment, a white batiste straight-jacket designed to flatten any unsightly bulges on our chests.

One year later, when I eventually finished my bloomers, they were too small and had to be given to a weedy class-mate, while I was marched off to the lingerie section of our local department store.

Believe it or not, after World War II, I actually made the layettes of my five children by hand, and on time. The point I am trying to make is—never denigrate the poor old sewing machine—consider it your third hand.

To get the right nostalgic feeling, all the quilts in this book have been sewn on a fifty-year-old Singer sewing machine I rescued from a second-hand shop.

Each quilt has a different story, from lighthearted nonsense to maternal anguish. I hope these patterns will help you to adapt your own designs to continue the age-old patchwork custom of holding up a mirror to your small part of the world.

MATERIALS

Try to keep away from haberdashery or fabric shops unless they are throwing out their remnants. Remember, the idea is to spend as little as you can. Inspect the wardrobes in your house and surreptitiously remove forgotten garments, but avoid synthetics and loosely-woven materials. Above all learn to see fabric in a different context. This mind game is enormously satisfying when you imagine that some garrulous acquaintance is actually wearing the 'roof of shark's mouth' . . . instead of a Giorgio Armani.

Never use a pattern or colour which will dominate, rather use one that will enhance your design, but alternatively don't be afraid to mix unexpected primary colours. If you look closely at some of these quilts you will see that I use a lot of materials in reverse, because when they are painted or tinted, the subdued pattern gives an added depth.

Now, after all this prattle, rush out and buy as much material as you can afford! It is one sure way of starting a worthwhile scrap bag.

TECHNIQUES

Build up your basic quilt first and then use this as the background for your individual piece-work appliqué. In patchwork piece-work the fabric pieces are actually incorporated into the quilt block. This is achieved by placing two right sides of fabric together and sewing with a narrow seam, so when opened out and ironed there is a flat seam on the front. However, most of the piece-work in the quilts throughout this book utilize curved shapes rather than straight lines, so ultimately they must be appliquéd to the quilt top. Curves are cut by placing the right side of the curved piece over the right side of the piece to be joined, and cutting a curve. Throw away the underneath piece and join the curved pieces together.

Begin each appliqué pattern by tracing the separate pieces onto the fabric, and cut them out, allowing for a seam. The seam allowance is turned under and machined with a black running stitch. Clip curved seam edges if necessary. Neaten the edges with black indelible marker pen. Now all these pieces are pinned to the main base shape and sewn in place. An example is the Mallee fowl* on the Country Homestead Quilt, which was a finished appliquéd piece before it was attached to the quilt background. At first this system may seem tedious, but it has three worthwhile advantages. It cuts down the number of pins needed when attaching it to the quilt or, in the case of a bird, gives you the opportunity to rearrange the feathers. It also gives the freedom to rearrange the design until you get the effect you want.

ASSEMBLY

If you are as hopeless at this as I am, then the only advice I can give you is to find a magic wand. But just in case you are determined, here is my method.

Firstly, there is the usual system of pinning the finished top, wadding and backing firmly together, and machine quilting with a loosened tension, from the centre out. I always have the backing 5cm (2in) wider all around than the top of the quilt. I evolved this system after laboriously hand-finishing the quilt from the back. On other occasions, depending on the design, I pad and quilt each section as I go. I also find it easier to quilt and back wide borders singly. Examples of this are the 'feather' and 'leaf' borders (p. 12 and p. 55). The centre of this type of quilt design is also backed and quilted separately, and then trimmed evenly all around.

The finished side borders are then joined to the centre and the extra 5cm (2in) used to neaten the seam at the back. Finally the top and bottom borders are added in the same manner. There is no question that hand-quilting is the ultimate finish, but such a leisurely pursuit is now too late for me. I should have persevered with hand-sewing way back in the early thirties.

PAINTING

This is a deceptively simple way to get an instant effect. Try painting a feather first. Cut out the feather shape with a 5mm ($^1/_4$in) seam, and dampen the shape with a clean water-colour brush. If it is a magpie feather, for example, flood the seam with a full brush of black fabric paint. This will gradually seep towards the centre of the feather. Control this seepage with a hot iron, if you want touches of white, or darken with more black paint. Another way is to dampen the centre of the feather and reverse the procedure.

Iron the shapes dry and draw the veins with an indelible marker. Turn the seam under and sew around in black. Neaten this edge with indelible marker. Soon you will become an adventurous fabric painter, but this is a subtle way of painting until you gain confidence. As you progress through the quilts, you will notice that detail and verve are easily achieved with the fabric paint and the humble black marker.

ADAPTATION OF TECHNIQUES USING DIFFERENT QUILT THEMES

Piece-work appliqué, where every object is finished separately, allows the design to be flexible and the appliquéd pieces to be handled without falling apart. It gives the freedom to rearrange designs while using the same or added components. Don't be anxious because you can't draw. Everybody can after a fashion and it is the primitive style that is appealing in folk art. Fortunately appliqué is a kind medium, which relies on sensitivity rather than perfect draftsmanship. With this in mind ask a child in your life or an adult with a naïve style to draw you a bird, animal, or flower. You will not feel awed when you enlarge their simple efforts. After drawings are created in cloth and their charms are apparent, it will encourage you to develop your own style. You may have to adapt careless tight lines into a broader style. Children, with their innocent desire to learn, accept these corrections, and it will help you gain confidence. An example of this is Sofia's Happy Garden Quilt (p. 37). Her little birds in the nest were impossible and had to be enlarged.

In the meantime secretly practise mental drawing. Trace the outline of everything you see carefully with your eyes then slowly add the details inside that perimeter. As you improve you will automatically block in the shadows, and this feeling for form will help your painting technique. It's just a question of practise—and doesn't cost a lot. ◩

---

* Mallee fowl: Native bird from the Mallee region, Victoria, Australia

SCRAPFLOWER
QUILT

My friend Elizabeth Brenchley is an ardent champion of Australian flora and fauna, with the exception of my favourite birds the currawongs and magpies. She calls them assassins because they have a playful habit of swooping on the smaller parakeets and honeyeaters who flock to her garden when the bottle-brush and gum blossom are in flower. My black-feathered friends can hardly be blamed if the silly little birds die of fright. She insists they are torn apart.

All this mayhem is happening right on the shores of Sydney Harbour. However not all her garden is devoted to Australian plants. She hid a few favoured exotic bushes down the side of the house, and was amazed when she went to tidy away the coloured paper napkins scattered over the bushes and found they were actually giant flowers. This couch quilt is their last laugh.

SCRAPFLOWER
QUILT

INSTRUCTIONS
Size approx. 1.5m (4ft 10in) x 1.3m (4ft 4in)

MATERIALS
3.6m (4yd) black cotton fabric for backing
90cm (1yd) black polyester/cotton fabric for binding
180cm (2yd) wadding
3.6m (4yd) blue cotton fabric for centre panel and border strips
180cm (2yd) yellow and 180cm (2yd) light green cotton fabric
90cm (1yd) each of a dark and medium green fabric
90cm (1yd) fabric for each of the four flower colours

This quilt, as its name suggests, should be made from multiple pieces of scrap material. Except for the black backing, mine was made entirely this way; the petals could even be crazy patchwork.

DIRECTIONS
There are only two pattern pieces: one leaf and one petal. The same shapes, large or small are used throughout. See illustration. The flower petals are padded and bound in black cotton fabric, then assembled and sewn together. The large petals are quilted with running stitch, the smaller ones decorated. The edges of the leaves and stems are turned under, sewn down and neatened with indelible marker. Use dark and light green fabric for leaves and stems.

BACKGROUND
Border the blue background with a 5cm (2in) strip of the light green cotton fabric. Pin the finished leaves and stems to the background. Sew in place. Next add the blue, yellow and black borders. Pin this top firmly to the wadding and backing. The backing is 5 cm (2in) wider all around than the top. Pin the flowers firmly in place and sew to the quilt top. Smooth out from the centre, re-pin and sew around the outside of the light green border. Turn the backing edge over and finish off the quilt. The appliquéd bumble bee is hiding an accidental splotch of red paint! ◧

134 cms
4' 4³/₄"

134 cms
4' 4³/₄"

There are two basic shapes to be used in this flower pattern.

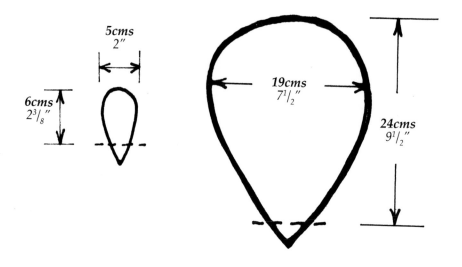

5cms
2"

6cms
2³/₈"

19cms
7¹/₂"

24cms
9¹/₂"

*The one basic shape, small and large,
to make the petals.*

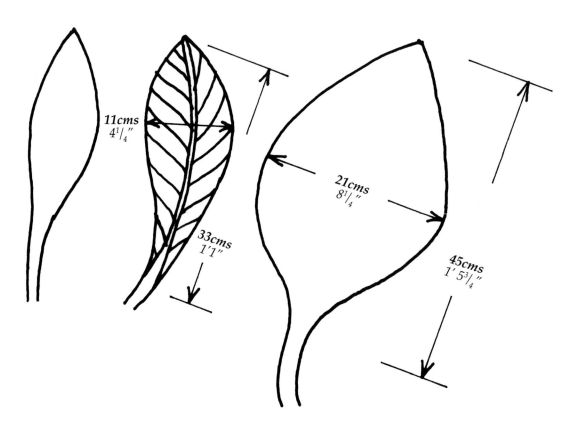

11cms
4¹/₄"

33cms
1'1"

21cms
8¹/₄"

45cms
1'5³/₄"

*These shapes are variations of the one shape
(some are reversed) to make the leaves.*

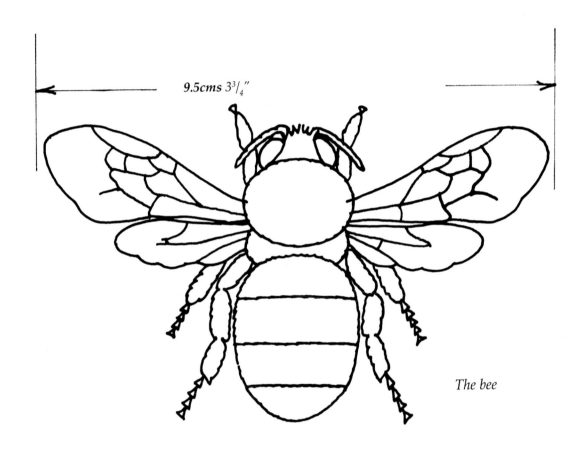

9.5cms 3³/₄″

The bee

166cms
5'5³/₈"

139cms
4'6³/₄"

WARATAH
QUILT

The Australian Aborigines called this magnificent scarlet flower Waratah, which means 'beautiful' in their tribal language. It is reported to be the only flower a black man ever gave a white man as a peace-offering. The colours in this quilt are an oblique salute to the past. Red, black and yellow are the colours of the Aboriginal flag.

INSTRUCTIONS
Size approx. 1.7m (5ft 6in) x 1.4m (4ft 8in)

MATERIALS
3.6m (4yd) black cotton fabric, backing and front
3.6m (4yd) wadding
90cm (1yd) black polyester/cotton fabric for binding
3.6m (4yd) dark green cotton fabric
2.75m (3yd) medium green cotton fabric
2.75 (3yd) yellow cotton fabric
3.6m (4yd) dark red polished cotton fabric; use either side or 180cm (2yd) each of different-coloured red cotton fabrics

You may have realised by now that I tend to over-estimate material quantities, as it is foreign for me to think in such an ordered manner. I juggle existing materials. (I even had the polished red cotton.)

DIRECTIONS
The secret of this simple pattern is to rearrange the basic pieces to give variety to each flower. See illustration. All pieces but the stems are bound in black and the veins of the leaves are drawn in indelible marker. Waratah leaves are serrated but I have simplifed this. The four sections of yellow background are approx 43 cm (17in) long by 37cm (14$\frac{1}{2}$in) wide. Unless you are a purist don't worry if your vertical joining strips are off centre. I don't.

BORDERS AND TEMPLATES
These are explained by the succinct illustration. These strip borders and templates can be arranged any way you like. The sawtooth pattern is similar to that found on Waratah leaves. Back and quilt. ◪

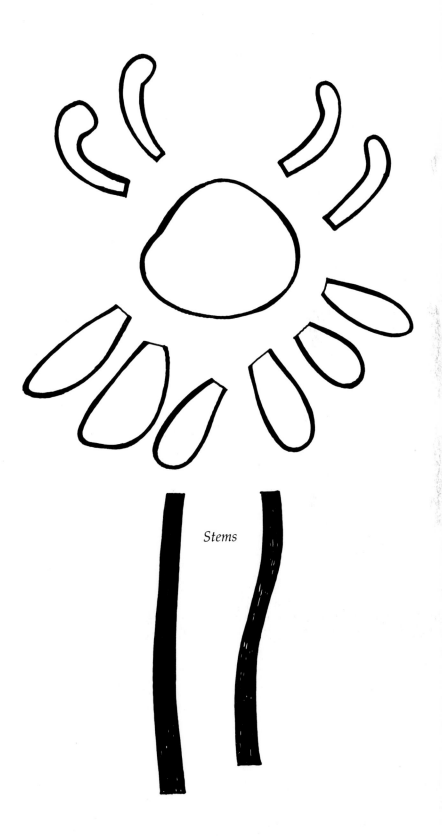

Stems

*All shapes can be reversed and used in different
combinations to create a different flower each time.*

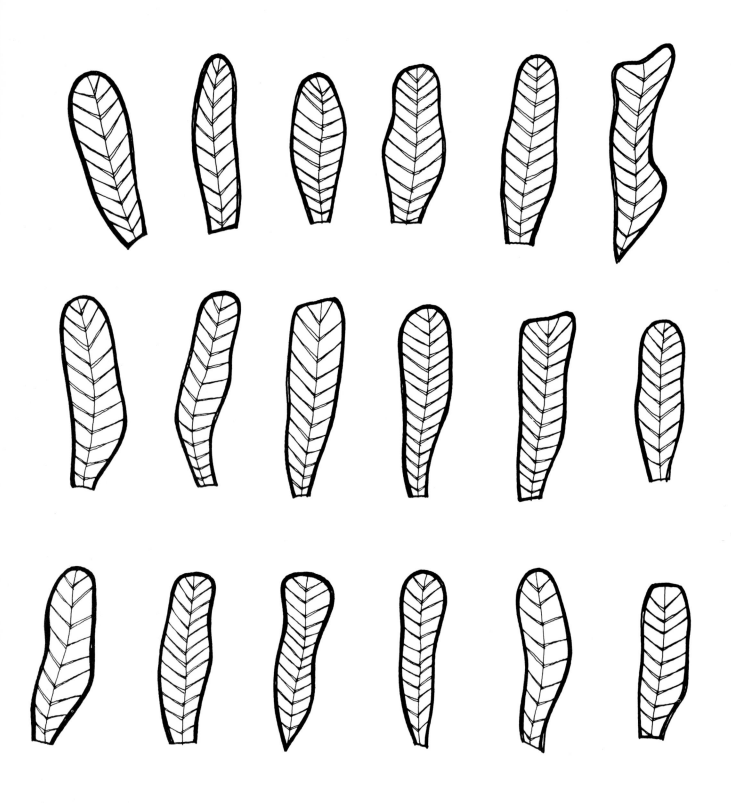

*All these leaf shapes have been used for the
Waratahs—use as many or as few as you wish.*

*Each panel measures **42cms** $1'4^1/_2''$ deep by **35cms** $1'1^3/_4''$ wide*

SUNFLOWER
QUILT

Van Gogh is a hard act to follow with sunflowers, but I will keep on trying for no other reason than the jubilant sound of the word sunflower. It is a universal flower loved by parrots and people all over the world.

Patterns from Bird's Quilt (p. 41) could be used with the flowers to create an entirely different effect. A bunch of sunflowers or a sunflower quilt is a joyful present.

SUNFLOWER
QUILT

INSTRUCTIONS
Size approx. 1.7m (5ft 6in) x 1.5m (5ft)

MATERIALS
4.5m (5yd) black cotton fabric for the back and front of
    the quilt
3.6m (4yd) wadding
90cm (1yd) blue cotton fabric
90cm (1yd) light green background cotton fabric
90cm (1yd) dark green fabric
90cm (1yd) medium green cotton fabric
46cm ($^1/_2$yd) grey cotton fabric for the stems
90cm (1yd) each of two different check materials

The sunflower colours can vary from 46cm ($^1/_2$yd) to
180cm (2yd) depending on whether you want to use the
colour in the border. Look through your scrap bag for
different greens and yellows.

DIRECTIONS

BACKGROUND
The finished centre panel is 115cm (45in) long by 1m
(38in) wide. The lower half of this is a curved green piece
66cm (26in) high. Divide this by a horizontal strip of
black from the top of the green. Then a vertical black
strip at the top and two at the bottom. See illustration.
Finish this panel off with a black border.

THE SUNFLOWERS
The sunflowers are added to this base. As usual, cut each
appliqué piece with a seam allowance, and sew edges in
matching thread. The flowers are assembled and sewn
before being attached to the background. The sunflower
centres are padded and bound.

    See illustration for assembling flowers, but as this is
a freeform design it is an ideal chance to make your own
arrangement. When everything is sewn in place, add
borders, back and quilt. ◪

122 cms
4'

98cms
3'2¹/₂"

DOG
MOUNTAIN
WEDDING
QUILT

The owners of the past and present canines recorded here are as diverse as a newspaper executive, a night-club owner and a Nobel Prize winner. Lion and Tiger were mastiffs who roamed the grounds of my family's home sometime in the last century. When we were very young my cousin and I spent many happy hours looking for their graves in the dogs' cemetery.

My pug and the bridal couple's shih-tzu appear to be on guard against the indolent Prince Utter and my dear old friend and neighbour Folly. This may seem a strange wedding present, but it is a bitter-sweet quilt sewn with love and irony, especially if you believe the only place to bury a dog is in your heart, or maybe a quilt.

DOG
MOUNTAIN
WEDDING
QUILT

INSTRUCTIONS
Size approx. 1.5m (5ft) x 1.3m (4ft 6in)

MATERIALS
4.5m (5yd) black cotton fabric for backing and front

90cm (1yd) black polyester/cotton fabric for binding

180 cm (2yd) wadding

46cm ($^1/_2$yd) white cotton fabric, and 46 cm ($^1/_2$yd) black and white print for the hairy dog. This material is used on the right side and also in reverse.

46 cm ($^1/_2$yd) each of cream, stone-coloured and oatmeal fabrics and three warmer versions of these colours

scrap-bag material for the quilt background; make sure you have enough plain materials to include the names of your favourite animals

DIRECTIONS
The quilt top is finished first and then pinned firmly to the wadding and backing.

See the illustrations for sewing the dogs, which are finished, painted and bound before being placed on the quilt and sewn down.

Finish off the quilt and then add the dog names with an indelible marker. I enjoyed that part. ◪

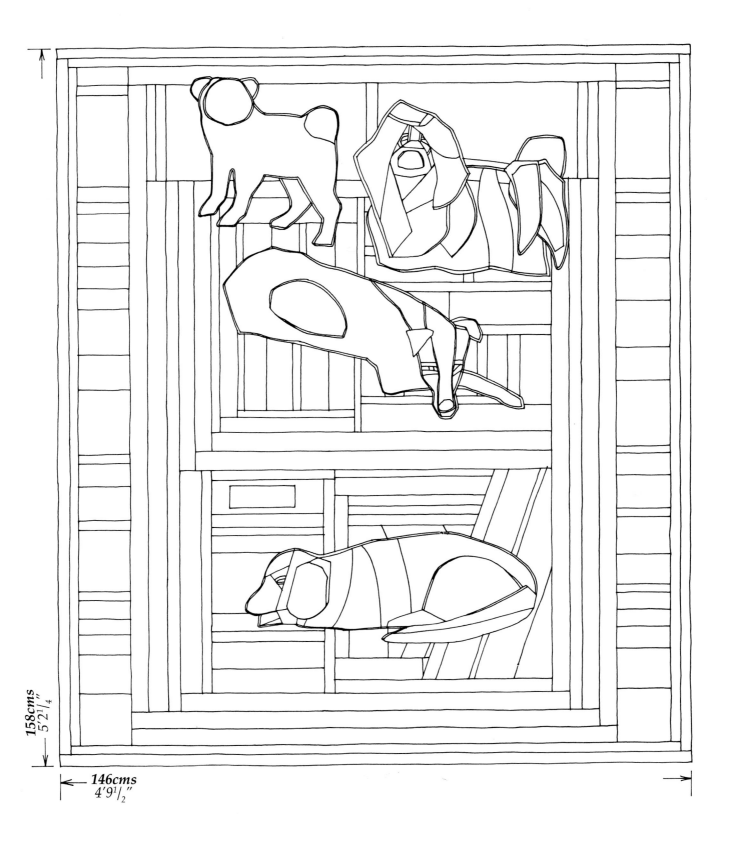

158cms
5'2¼"

146cms
4'9½"

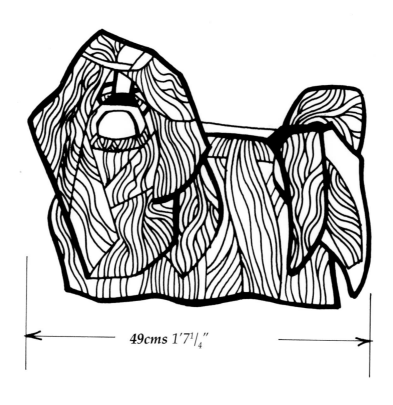

49cms $1'7^{1}/_{4}''$

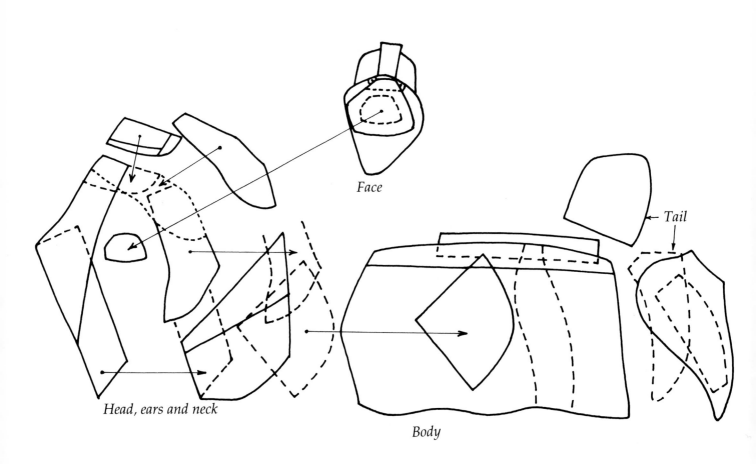

Face

Head, ears and neck

Body

Tail

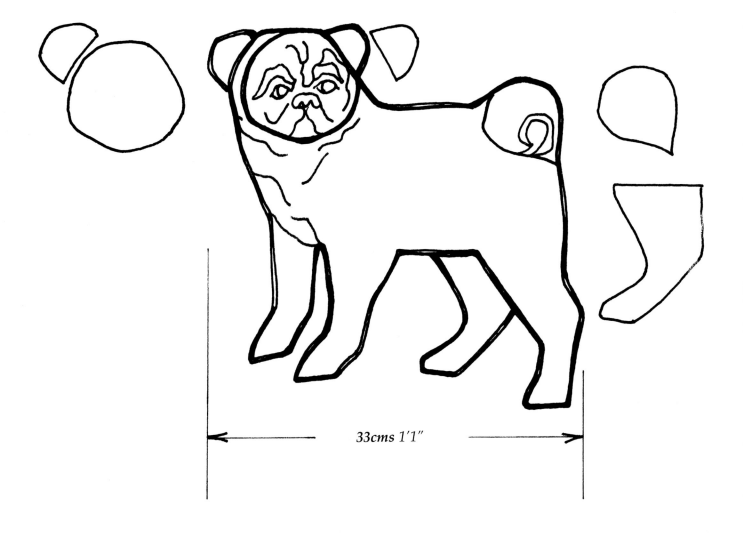

33cms 1'1"

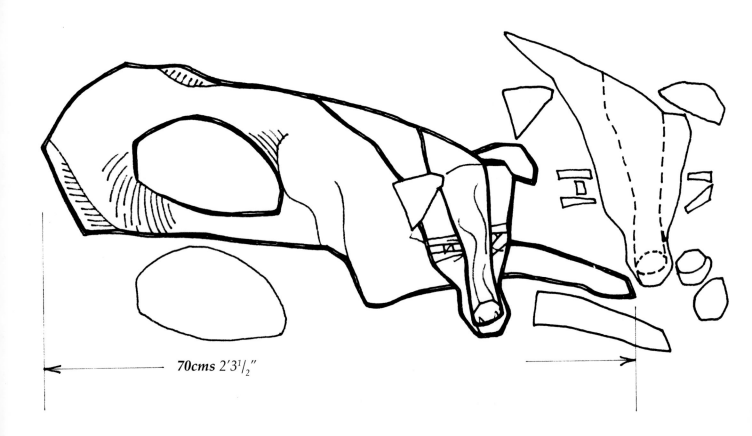

70cms 2'3$^1/_2$"

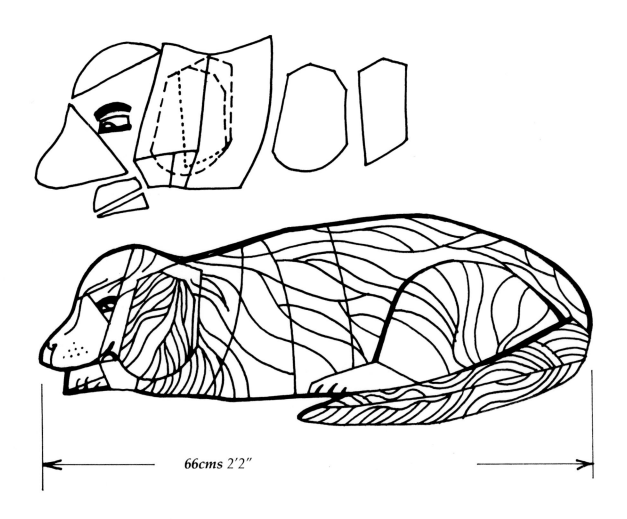

66cms 2'2"

PUG
QUILT

This was the couch quilt I used when I was lolling around watching television. It was the first of a series intended to use all my scrap material, but needless to say this frenzy didn't last long.

In 1988 my actress daughter Kate Fitzpatrick returned to Sydney to do a television series 'The Last Resort'. For the next 14 months MY quilt and MY pug Banjo spent most of the time on her bed. Before Katie returned to London I added the three pugs to the quilt to keep her warm in the Old Dart and remind her of distant shores. The pug artists were her nephew, niece, and mother, who live in San Diego, Jerusalem and Sydney respectively.

In case the catlovers become incensed, I will now tell you some cat stories. When I was twelve my first and last feline love was a glowing creature called Titian who slept on my bed and gave me presents. His most spectacular offering was a half-eaten rat. One morning I woke up and found Titian dead on the rug. He had been savaged by a dog and crawled in my window to die. Since then the only cats in my life have been a succession of strays dragged home by my children.

These starving, half-drowned specimens became sleek and crafty and were named Pooh Bear, Honey Fitz, Shamrock Hilton and Chilla. They not only endured 'trips to the moon' from the top of bunk beds, but Chilla actually survived a four-storey fall from the top of an apartment building. Finally, being astute cats, they hunted out lonely old ladies who changed their names to Alice or Roland and allowed them to visit the Fighting Fitzs when their boredom became intolerable.

PUG

QUILT

INSTRUCTIONS
Size approx. 1.4m (4ft 8in) x 1.3m (4ft 5in)

MATERIALS
3.6m (4yd) black cotton fabric for backing and front of quilt
180cm (2yd) wadding
180cm (2yd) yellow cotton fabric for border strips
180cm (2yd) natural cotton fabric for pugs
180cm (2yd) calico
all other materials from the scrap bag

DIRECTIONS
See illustration for measurements of panels and template border. The quilt centre is done in three sections and joined together by black strips. There is no set rule—crazy patchwork is my favourite pattern because it has the gutsy and gaudy feeling of a circus background, which makes it ideal for appliquéd objects. A traditional template border makes order out of the chaos.

THE PUGS
See illustrations. The manner of assembling these little dogs applies to cats, rabbits or even a tortoise. (We had a tortoise called Water-lily who wandered away from the safety of her pond and was flattened by a bus. That gratuitous information is to dispel the implication that only pugs should sit on quilts.) This type of quilt is not meant for the Royal Show or County Fair, but to invoke family memories and private jokes. It is also a relaxed way of involving children who love helping. My four-year-old grandson Felix recently helped me print the scales on a crocodile with a potato cut. In the end we had more mashed potatoes than scales.

Place the finished quilt on top of the wadding and backing, pin firmly. Quilt down the black strips. Then add the pugs. Finish off in the usual manner. ◪

142cms
4'8"

136cms
4'5¹/₂"

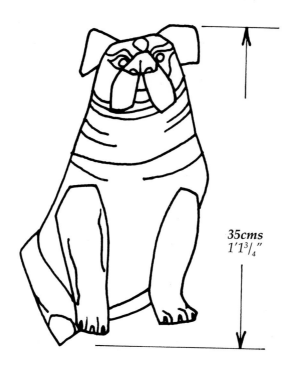

35cms
1'1³/₄"

*See breakdown of dogs on Dog Mountain Wedding Quilt
(p.22-25) for the method of assembling small animals.*

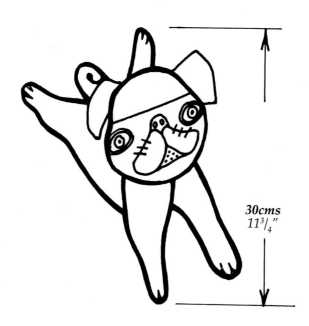

30cms
11³/₄"

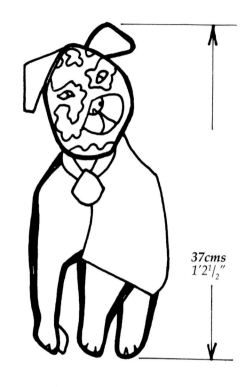

37cms
$1'2^1/_2''$

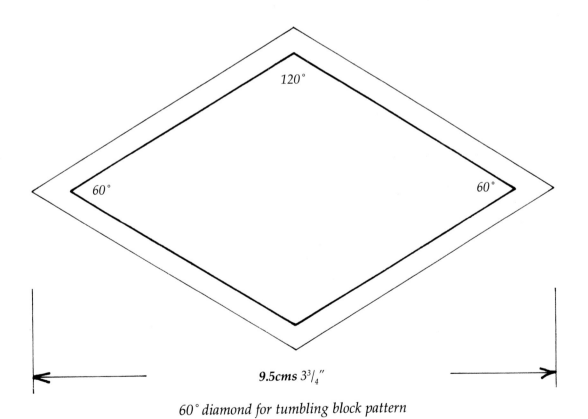

120°

60°   60°

9.5cms $3^3/_4''$

60° diamond for tumbling block pattern

133cms
4'4³/₈"

150cms
4'11"

164cms
5'4¹/₂"

150cms
4'11"

SOFIA'S HAPPY GARDEN

QUILT

The original drawing of this quilt was a Father's Day present to my eldest son, from his eldest daughter. She was six at the time. Most of us have torn or crumpled treasures like this hidden away after their days of glory on the refrigerator door are over.

The only problem with this type of sentimental couch quilt is keeping it out of the hands of the original artist, especially if she is now fifteen, and has a black belt in karate. Begin while the children are young. A small quilt for the new baby made from the drawings of older siblings is a perfect 'family' gift.

INSTRUCTIONS
Size approx. 1.7m ($5^1/_2$ft) x 1.5m (5ft)

MATERIALS
3.6m (4yd) black cotton fabric for backing
90cm (1yd) black polyester/cotton fabric for binding
180cm (2yd) wadding
3.6m (4yd) fabric for background colour
180cm (2yd) calico
90cm (1yd) each of the other colours for the large flowers
   —see how much you can get out of your scrap bag

DIRECTIONS
There is no need for detailed instructions to complete the flowers and trees. The illustration is self-explanatory. The two-tone bush in the centre is bound in black and decorated with indelible marker. The outline of all the other objects is turned under and stitched.

THE SUN AND THE SKY
I have always been fascinated by the way young children paint the sky firmly against the top of the page. It is a wonderful concept, as if they are tugging down the hat brim of the Universe. This no-nonsense attitude is balanced by the grass blades at the bottom of the quilt.

To Ben.
This is for
your father's
Day Present

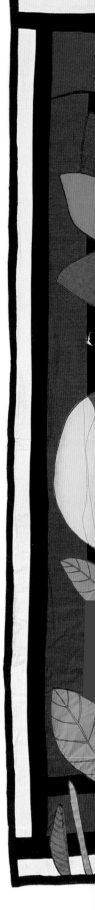

SOFIA'S HAPPY GARDEN

QUILT

BIG BIRD, LITTLE BIRDS, INSECTS AND WORMS

See illustrations for these. Trace drawings of the little birds and insects onto white material, paint and draw details. When handling small appliqué, cut the outer seam allowance larger than usual; this makes it easier to handle. Sew down outline and trim. Use the same drawings of small creatures in reverse if you want to fill up spaces.

THE BACKGROUND

The centre panel measures approx 1.3m (54in) by 1.1m (44in). On either side of this sew a 4cm (1$^1/_2$in) strip of black and a 7cm (3in) strip of the centre panel. Use this in reverse if it is one of those fabrics with a darker background. Border the bottom with another strip of black and the centre colour. Pin the finished sky in position and sew down.

Next add, in sequence, the large flowers and trees. You will have assembled these in the usual manner, with their detail drawn. The line work on the flowers is machine running stitch. The petal edges are detailed by indelible marker. The nest of little birds is completed next and sewn to the big tree before being attached to the background. The big bird with his beak of worms is also completely finished before he is sewn in place. Add the insects, little bird and other worms. Take a rest.

Now sew another black strip and a 5cm (2in) calico strip to either side. Across the bottom and top add a 5cm (2in) black and a 5cm (2in) calico strip.

At some stage you will have prepared all the little grass shoots. Now pin these along the bottom ends of the calico and sew in place. See illustration. Use different greens for the shoots.

BACKING

Pin the top very firmly to the wadding and backing, which as usual is 5cm (2in) wider all around. Quilt with a loose tension as many of these objects as you wish. After this struggle, turn the backing over the calico and finish off the quilt. At this stage you will wish you had torn up the little beast's drawing years ago. ◪

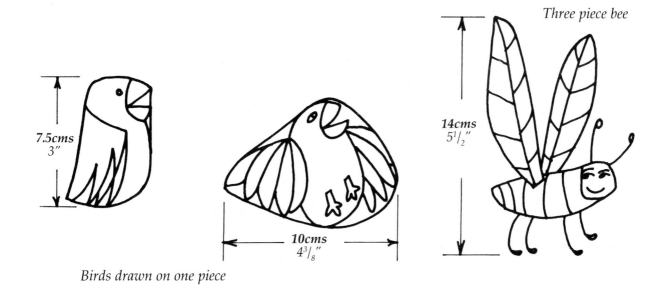

7.5cms
3"

10cms
4$^3/_8$"

14cms
5$^1/_2$"

Three piece bee

Birds drawn on one piece

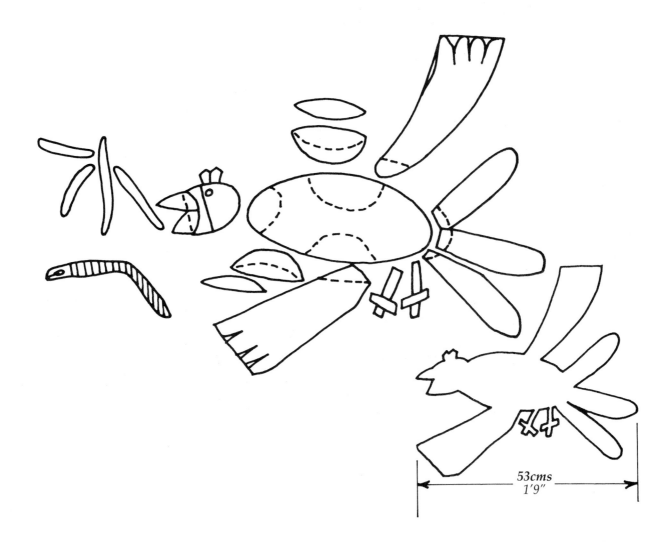

53cms
1'9"

BIRD'S
QUILT

After I discovered some crude little birds and branches in the scrap bag—discarded for obvious reasons—I decided to use them as a permanent reminder that my former 'oversew' method was ugly and insensitive.

A quilt like this is a simple and effective way to involve children in design. It is also a lesson in how to recycle your failures. The fierce little 'Messerschmidts' in the top left-hand corner were drawn straight onto the yellow fabric by a nine-year-old neighbour, Charles. My tracing of his drawing, without the scribble and splosh, is the little white bird flying towards them. You must always look beyond the Jackson Pollock painting style of young children for spontaneous designs.

To appease the cat lovers, my granddaughter's feral cat is licking his chops at the base of the tree. This quilt is owned by my third son Justin who is still known in the family by his childhood name of Bird.

BIRD'S
QUILT

INSTRUCTIONS
Size approx. 1.5m (5ft) x 1.46m (4ft 10in)

MATERIALS
6.4m (7yd) black cotton fabric for backing and the tree
90cm (1yd) black polyester/cotton fabric for binding
   black birds
3.6m (4yd) cotton fabric for centre panel
140cm (1$^1/_2$yd) each of three border colours
46cm ($^1/_2$yd) each of two different greens
use the scrap bag for extra colours

DIRECTIONS

TREE AND BACKGROUND
Prepare the quilt top. See large illustration. Place this on the wadding and backing. The tree and branches are done with scissor-drawing. This dangerous practice means cutting the shapes (see illustration) from the fabric without a pattern. It's not only quick, but quite exhilarating. Turn under the various edges and neaten. Assemble the tree. Do not worry about an exact copy. Pin the tree firmly to the background and sew in place. Now you will have a stable foundation to add the various birds etc. But do not forget, as the background is semi-quilted, each new object must be sewn to the background from the centre outwards. Smooth as you go. When all the birds are in place, turn the extra backing over the quilt top and sew down.

THE KINGFISHER, FISH AND TREE TRUNK
See illustration. This bird is easy in spite of his painted face. The three pieces are bound and padded before being sewn together.

THE COCKATOO
He is also simple. See illustration. Enlarge the design and trace onto material. Draw with indelible marker. If you can find different self-patterned white materials the result is richer. His yellow feathers are painted.

THE CURRAWONGS OR MAGPIES
The same head, face and foot pattern is used for these three birds. The pattern can also be reversed. Join a piece of white cotton fabric to the black side before you cut out the main shape. See illustration. Pin the tracing paper to this and trace the beak, head outline and eye onto the white fabric. Cut out the shape leaving the usual seam allowance. Turn this under, sew down and paint the head.

The painting of feathers are discussed on page 1 and page 52. See illustration for different ways of placing them on the body shape. Use this technique for any bird.

THE SEAGULL
Only four pieces: body, 2 wings and foot. See illustration. Paint shadows, beak and eye.

THE PARROT
When handling small scraps of material, piece them together first in their general sequence, making sure you have a white piece for the (beak-face) head. Place the pattern on this, shifting to the best position, and trace the outline and details. Cut out shape with seam allowance, neaten edge. Paint face and beak.

This broad approach eliminates trying to handle tiny scraps of material. It also applies to any other multiple coloured pieced shapes. The illustration gives a precise method.

THE BANKSIA FLOWERS AND CONES
Use the reverse of a black and white fabric for the cones and the right side for the nuts. Tint these brown/grey. For the split-nut effect join two pieces of the dark side of the material with a narrow orange strip. Cut the nut shape from this, tint, turn under edge and sew down. Use the reverse of the same material for the flower base, neaten edges and tint. Cut short strips of fraying material, sew these down the centre to the flower base. Trim and fray. Thai silk is ideal for this as the warp and the weft give different colours. ◰

140cms
4'7"

157.5cms
5'2"

161cms
5'3¹/₂"

148cms
4'10¹/₄"

Reverse the body for a different direction

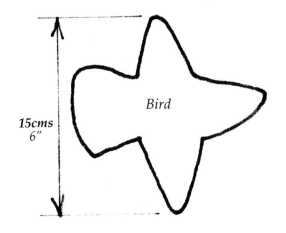

15cms
6″

Bird

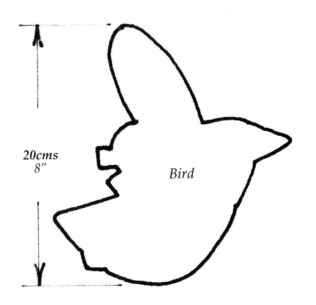

20cms
8"

Bird

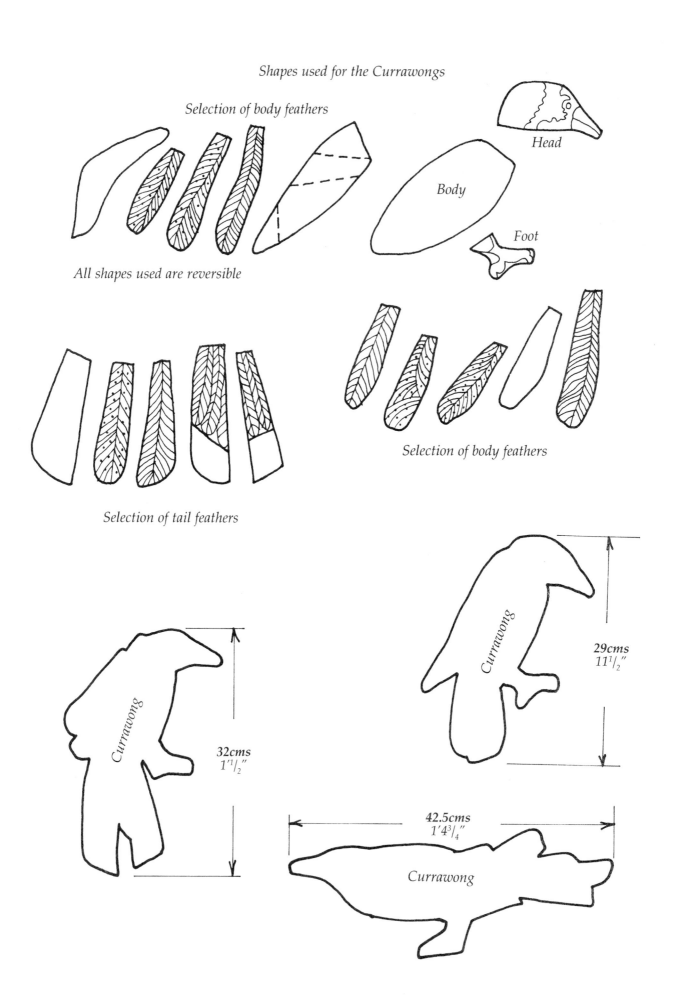

Shapes used for the Currawongs

Selection of body feathers

Head

Body

Foot

All shapes used are reversible

Selection of tail feathers

Selection of body feathers

Currawong

32cms
1'1½"

Currawong

29cms
11½"

Currawong

42.5cms
1'4¾"

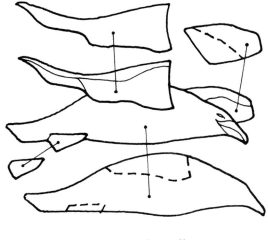

Seagull

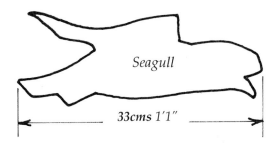

Seagull

33cms 1'1"

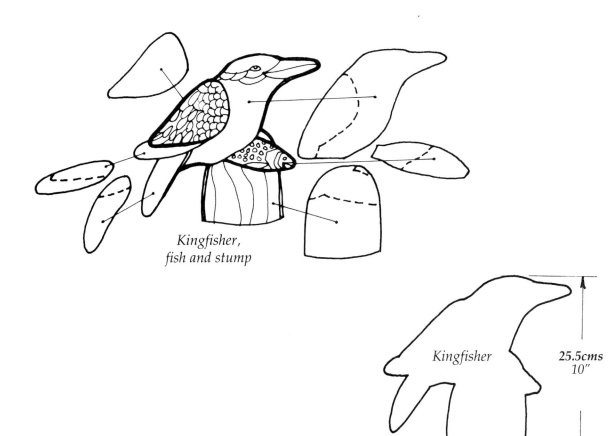

*Kingfisher,
fish and stump*

Kingfisher

25.5cms
10"

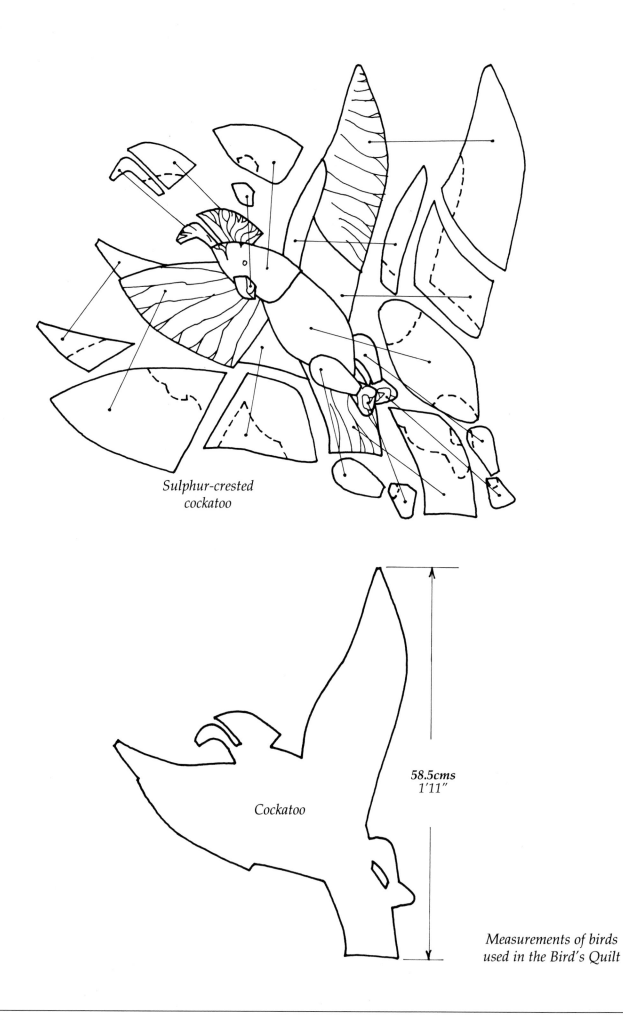

Sulphur-crested
cockatoo

Cockatoo

58.5cms
1'11"

Measurements of birds
used in the Bird's Quilt

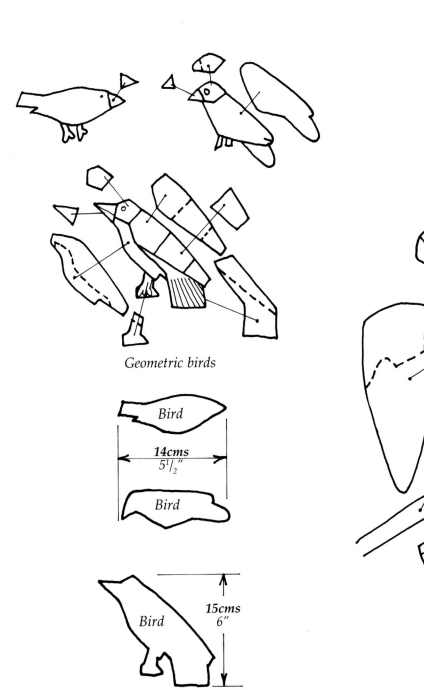

Geometric birds

Bird

14cms
$5^1/_2''$

Bird

Bird

15cms
6"

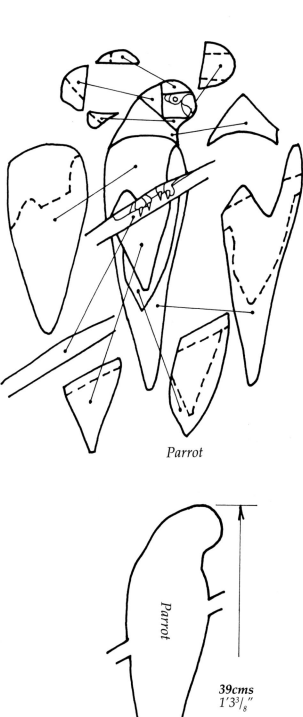

Parrot

Parrot

39cms
$1'3^3/_8''$

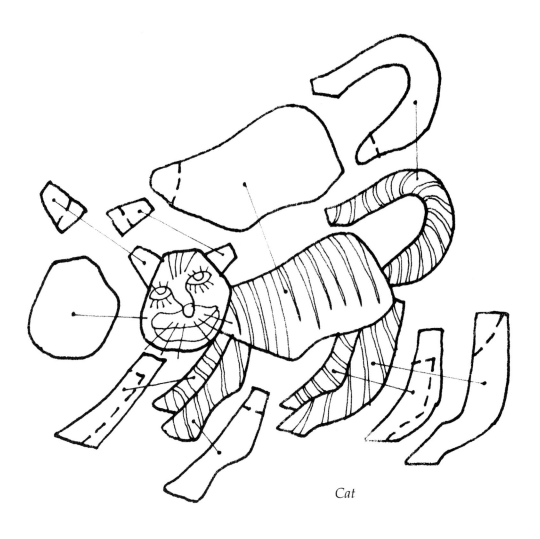

Cat

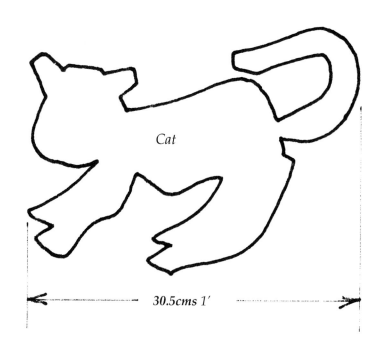

Cat

30.5cms 1'

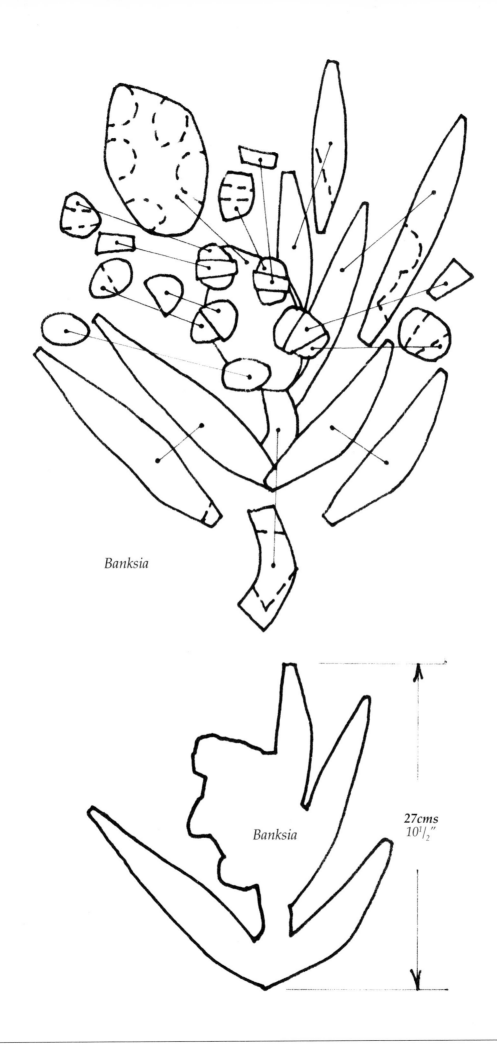

Banksia

Banksia

27cms
10$\frac{1}{2}$"

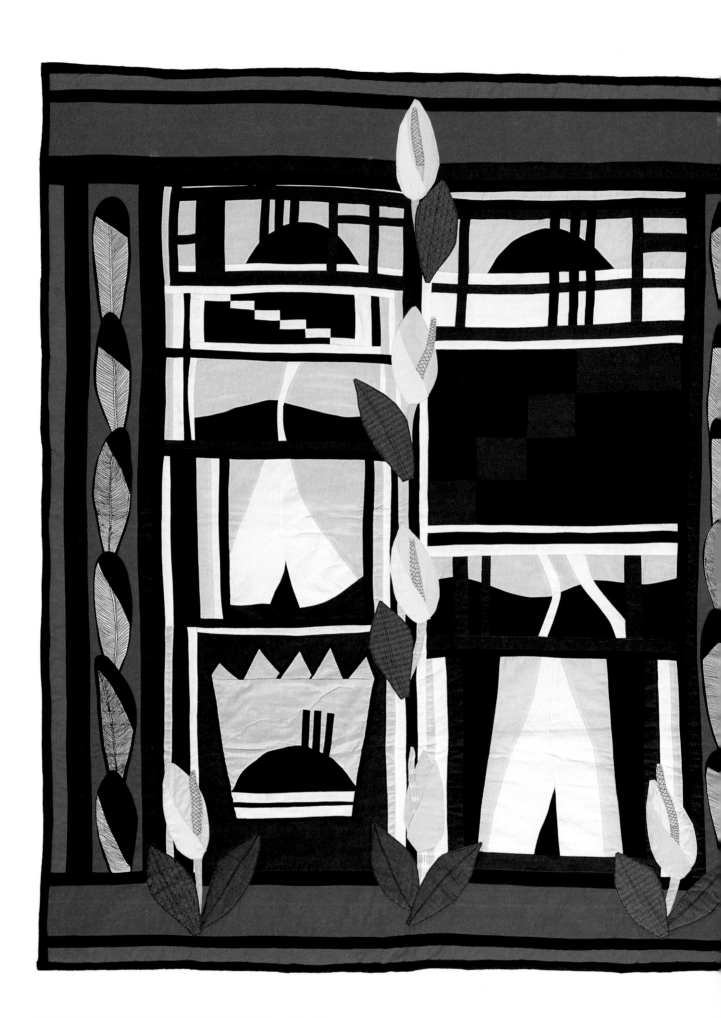

WINTER SOLSTICE
QUILT

At first glance this may seem a straightforward design based on an American Indian theme but it also has a message for my daughter Sally who lives in San Diego with her husband and sons and boxer dog. Sal loves the mountains and the Hopi Indians. In 1989, while the family were away on a mountain trek, a gas explosion wrecked the house, blew her car 50 metres down the street, and incinerated my wall-hanging of the American Presidents' Wives, which was stored in her garage. I thought it might make her feel better to know it is now safely in the great White Tepee in the sky, instead of the White House.

WINTER SOLSTICE

INSTRUCTIONS

Size approx. 1.75m (5ft 9in) x 1.45m (4ft 9in)

MATERIALS

5.5m (6yd) black cotton fabric for front and backing of
    quilt
3.6cm (4yd) wadding
2.75m (3yd) white cotton fabric
3.6m (4yd) dark green cotton fabric
2.75m (3yd) ice-green cotton fabric
90 cm (1yd) each of dark and light yellow cotton fabric
    for the lilies; the stamens and stems can be cut from
    white cotton fabric and tinted
2.75m (3yd) dark red cotton fabric and 1.4m ($1^1/_2$yd) of
    light red cotton fabric
90cm (1yd) medium green cotton fabric

DIRECTIONS

Start with the Hopi design in the lower left-hand corner.
This will familiarize you with the other sections which
are only variations of the same theme. There are five
designs on the left-hand side and four on the right side.
Study the illustration for enlarging these sections by
grid. Sew each design separately and join together.

The mountain and sky are joined by a curve, then a
curve is cut through the middle and the white smoke
inserted. The black verticals of the Hopi design, which
are also repeated at the top of the quilt, are appliquéd.
When finished the two sides are joined by a 2.5cm (1in)
black strip. The feathers are white cotton with black
cotton tips. They are bound in black and then tinted and
drawn with indelible marker. Assemble the side borders
and sew on the feathers, then join them to the centre
panel. Assemble and attach the top and bottom borders.
Pin the top to the wadding and backing, then quilt. See
illustration for lilies. Complete sewing before attaching
to quilt top. Finally turn the extra backing over the front
edge and sew down. ◪

174cms
5'8¹/₂"

149cms
4'10⁵/₈"

*Build each separate design to the same size
with vertical and horizontal strips, then join the
completed left and right sides by a centre seam.*

Hopi design

174cms
5'8¹/₂"

149cms
4'10⁵/₈"

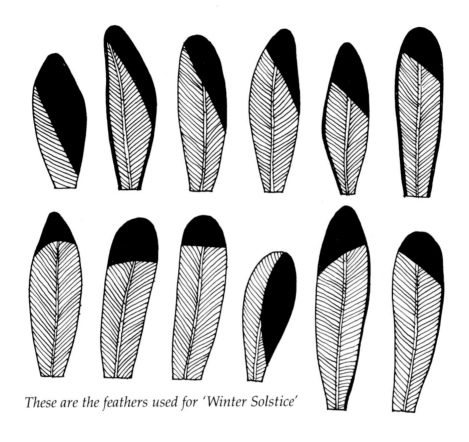

These are the feathers used for 'Winter Solstice'

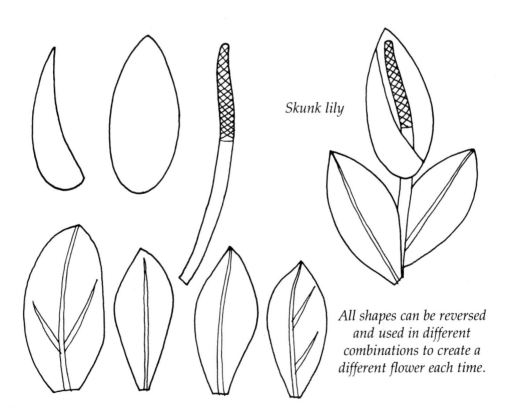

Skunk lily

All shapes can be reversed and used in different combinations to create a different flower each time.

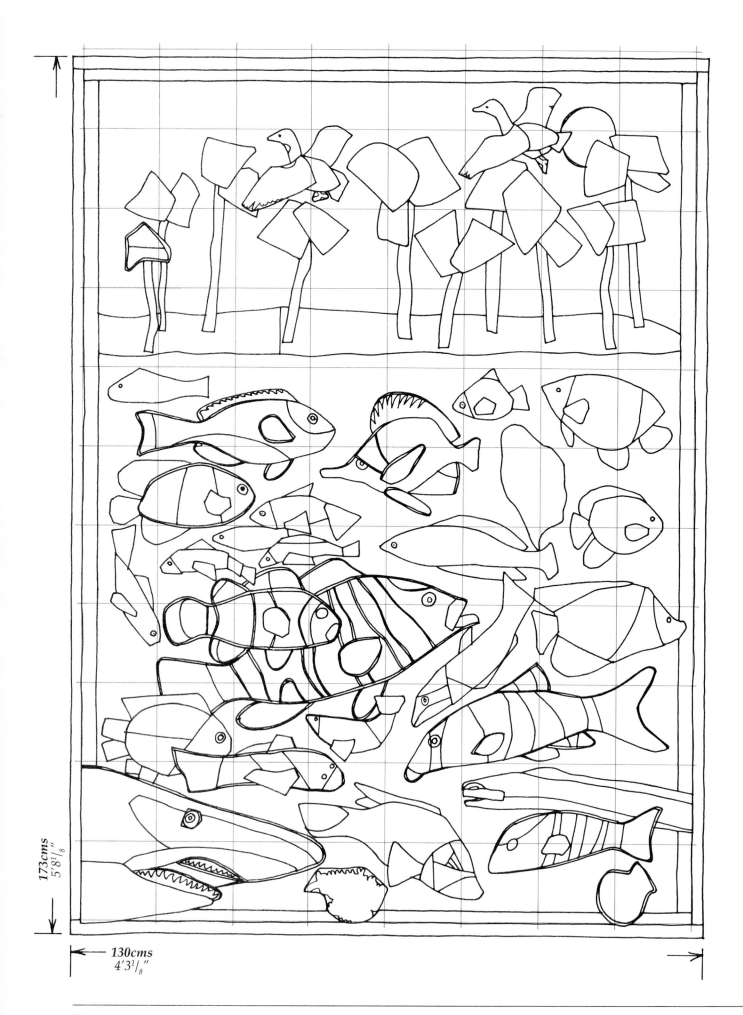

173cms
5'8¹/₈"

130cms
4'3¹/₈"

CORAL SEA

QUILT

This was designed as a wall-hanging for the marble-floored entrance hall of a luxurious Queensland coastal apartment. However, just in case there is another Stock Market crash it can be taken down and used as a summer quilt to take the chill off the tropical air.

INSTRUCTIONS
Size approx. 1.75m (5ft 9in) x 1.3m (4ft 3in)

MATERIALS
5.5m (6yd) black cotton fabric, backing and front

2.75m (3yd) striped cotton fabric for the sea. Cut in half. Join the two pieces down the side. The strips of the sea are horizontal.

1.4m (1$^1/_2$yd) yellow cotton fabric for the sky

46cm ($^1/_2$yd) green fabric for the island; cut in strips and join

90cm (1yd) each of three different black and white materials

90cm (1yd) white cotton fabric

The individual fish are made from scrap material.

DIRECTIONS

ISLAND
Curve the top of the green 'island' under and sew to the bottom of the yellow sky. Add a curved piece of calico, 2cm (1in), to the bottom of the island. Sew down the sun, trees and ducks. When the striped sea and fish are finished, sew these two pieces together. Press. Place on backing 4cm (2in) wider than the top. Turn over the edge and finish off.

CORAL SEA

QUILT

THE FLYING DUCKS

Enlarge ducks. Trace wings with feather design onto white cotton. Use the same procedure with head and foot. The body and tail are cut from two different black materials. Cut each piece with a seam allowance. Paint wings, head and foot. Sew down seams and assemble bird. See illustration.

THE TREES

The trees are the right side of a black and white material. The foliage is tinted green and the trunks brown. Finish all the little trees, and the sun. Pin them in place on the quilt top and sew down.

THE FISH

Turn to the illustrations for these. They are an exercise in the use of fabrics. Three examples of using the right and reverse side of fabrics are the shark, the mean-faced fish in front of him and the pale fish just above the seashell. So select materials with this thought in mind. Remember these fish are meant to be poetic illusions, not photographic replicas.

PAINTED FINISHES TO FISH

There are two ways of painting the eye(s) and mouth. Draw them directly onto a pale or white patch of the reversed material, or sew a piece of white cotton fabric across 'the face' of the body shape, draw in the eye and mouth, trim this to match the outline, turn under the seam and sew down. Paint or tint this to match the body colour. There is one fish half-way down the right hand side that gives the illusion of swimming through the water. His body was a thin striped green and white material, painted with blue wavy lines to match the background colour. Experiment to create your own individual style. ◪

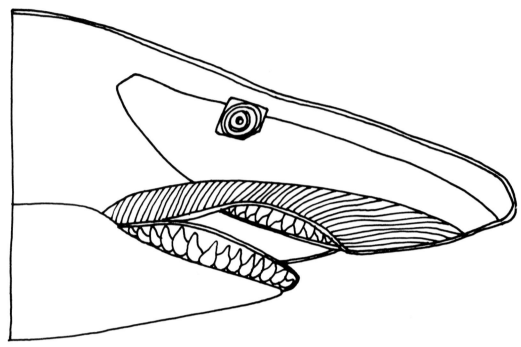

Shark

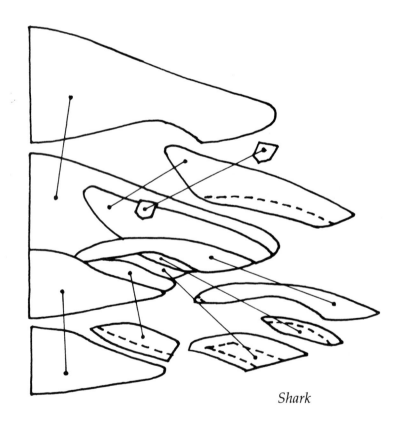

Shark

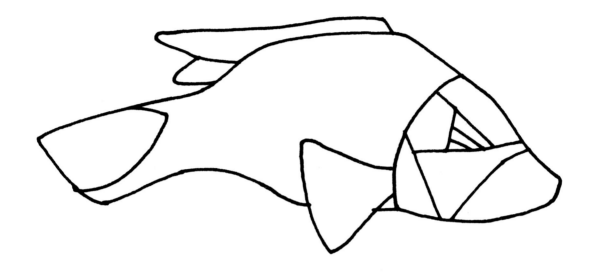

Head of groper

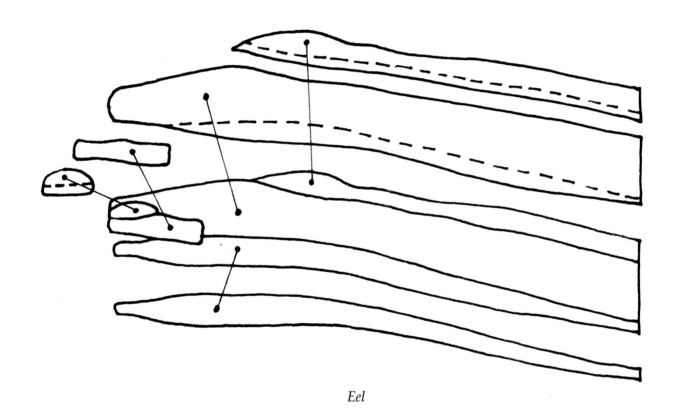

Eel

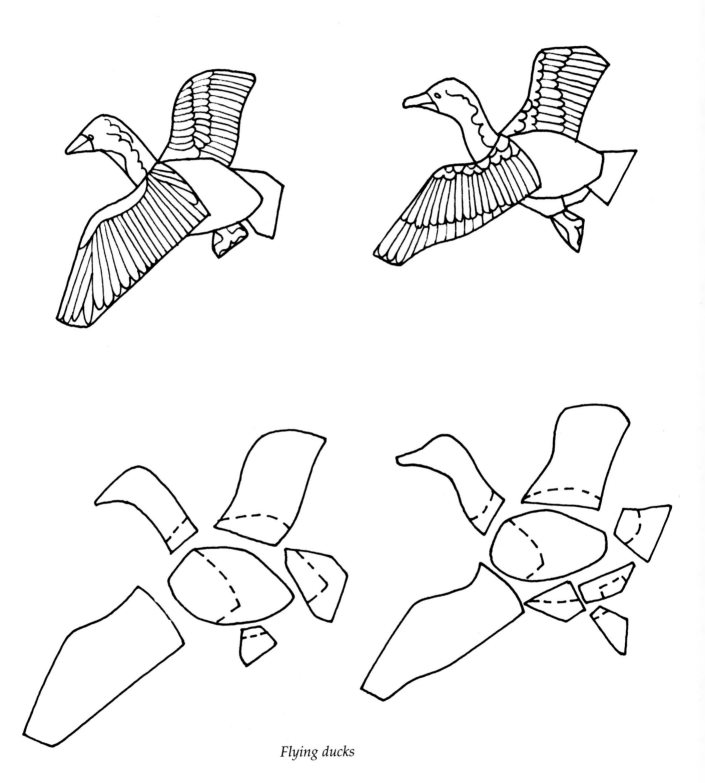

Flying ducks

181.5cms
5'11¹/₂"

145.5cms
4'9¹/₄"

BOOKCASE
QUILT

If you want to simplify your life, save money, and avoid lugging five crates of books every time you move, then this is the solution. Make yourself a bookcase quilt of all your favourite titles, hang it on the wall, and join the local library. This quilt is one of three hangings used for the stage play 'Stevie', by Hugh Whitemore. On the bottom shelf Fang the poodle belongs to the director, and the dog plate belongs to my pug.

INSTRUCTIONS
Size approx. 1.8m (6ft) x 1.5m (5ft)

MATERIALS
5.5m (6yd) black cotton fabric for the backing and quilt front, and binding
180cm (2yd) dark blue cotton fabric
3.6m (4yd) wadding
180cm (2yd) of a mottled dark brown fabric
90cm (1yd) white cotton fabric
90cm (1yd) each of two other shades of brown fabric

THE SCRAP BAG
Use this for the books and various objects. The flowers in the vase are cut from floral material. The vase is hand painted. The epergne of fruit is hand painted, but you may have material printed with fruit, grapes etc. You may even find some material printed with ships; cut one out and appliqué it onto a bottle shape. I have even seen material printed with books. There is no end to re-cycling existing images in appliqué.

BOOKCASE

QUILT

DIRECTIONS

THE BOOKCASE

This is not as complex as it looks. It is put together in four panels, so quilt these as you go.

I started on the tightly-packed second row. Books are either tall, fat, short or thin rectangles. These shapes are individually sewn with a curved top to the dark blue background shadow. See illustration for ideas for making them look different (e.g. torn dust-covers etc). When you have enough books sew them together in a straight line. You could leave a gap of the dark blue between the books, and afterwards appliqué ornaments or a stack of untidy books in the gap. When each shelf is finished cut a piece of wadding the same size, and quilt that shelf. This procedure means that when all the shelves are joined together, the quilt top only needs to be sewn to the backing in straight lines. If you have a pet cat, add it to the bookshelf, or any other favourite objects.

Finish off each shelf with a 2.5cm (1in) strip of black fabric at the top and 2.5cm (1in) strip of one of the browns at the bottom. When the shelves are finally sewn together the black creates a shadow.

The stacks of books are finished and bound and then sewn on top of each other. The names of the books are written in indelible marker. When I made this quilt I actually padded each one of those objects separately, as well as the background. ◪

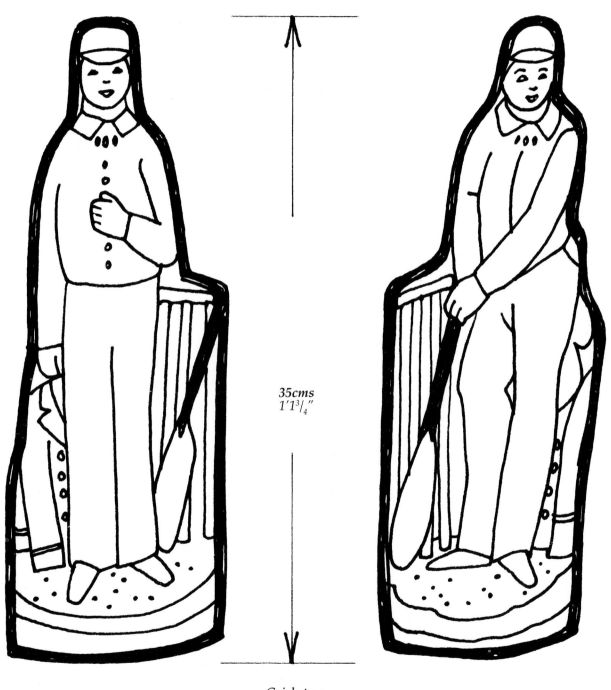

35cms
1'1³/₄"

Cricketers

Poodle

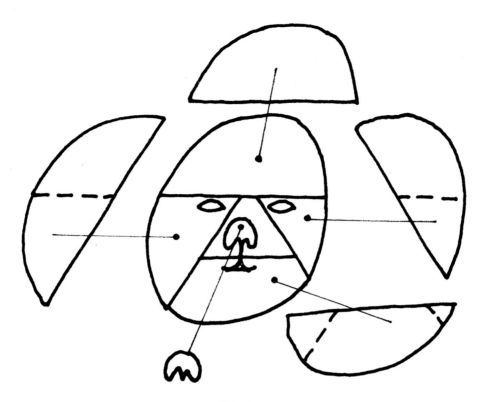

Poodle's face

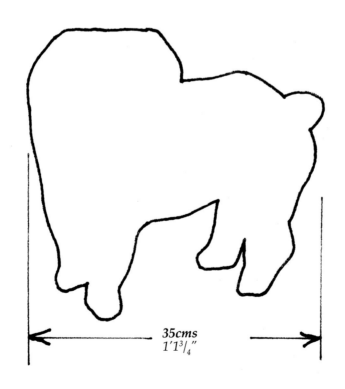

35cms
1'1³/₄"

173cms
5'8"

145cms
4'9"

MOTH

QUILT

Birthday quilts are wonderful to receive and satisfying to make. In the case of Julian's 21st birthday present I began by creating an imaginary mangrove swamp around the stunning parrot he drew as a nine-year-old. Behind the mangrove roots is a romantic version of my favourite city, Jerusalem. This amused me because he is studying architecture and is an avowed modernist. During a certain time of the year moths swarm in the millions across our state; twenty-one of them landed on this quilt! The concept of this design is flexible as the method allows you to substitute your own favourite city or town with another small person's drawing.

INSTRUCTIONS
Size approx. 1.7m (5ft 6in) x 1.5m (5ft)

MATERIALS
4.5m (5yd) black cotton fabric for backing and front
180cm (2yd) calico
180cm (2yd) wadding
90cm (1yd) white lawn for moths
90cm (1yd) Dshuti (a firm calico) for buildings and
  mangrove roots
3.6m (4yd) black and white printed cotton fabric—this
  is used in reverse for the background
90cm (1yd) each of the border colours; these will need to
  be joined

MOTH
QUILT

DIRECTIONS

This is painted appliqué, with the exception of the building in the lower right-hand corner, which has some appliqué. Cut a simple outline shape, leaving a seam allowance. Turn this under and sew down. See illustration. Paint buildings. If you limit your primary colours you will get interesting tonal effects mixing various colours. Cut the Dshuti panels to the size given on the illustrations. Tint and iron the mangrove air roots. Pin the various finished components to each panel and sew down. Also paint and draw the leaves and flowers. Mix quite an amount of the background wash and tint the background and the borders around the buildings. Control this with a hot iron to prevent it seeping into the painted pieces.

MANGROVE FLOWERS AND AIR ROOTS

Cut curving strips for the air roots; sew the edges under and tint. Trace mangrove leaves and flowers onto white cotton fabric (see illustration). Then paint. Draw the detail with indelible marker. Cut out the shape. Turn the edges under as near to the leaves etc. as possible, sew down the outside edge. Fill in the gaps with indelible marker. Arrange all these components in position. See illustration.

THE MOTHS

Trace the moths onto the lawn, paint and iron dry. Draw detail with indelible marker. When the outline of the moth has been sewn down, fill in any gaps around the wings with indelible marker and also the sewing edge.

THE PARROT, NEST, ANTS AND
MANGROVE SHOOTS

These details are treated the same way as everything else. However you might like to use some young artist's drawing instead of this parrot, so the illustration will give you an idea of how to assemble your bird. The ants are traced directly onto the shoots. After everything is sewn onto this panel, tint the background.

Join the six panels. See illustration. Place the finished top on the wadding and backing and quilt as usual. ◪

*These are the moth patterns that have
to be used in the Moth Quilt*

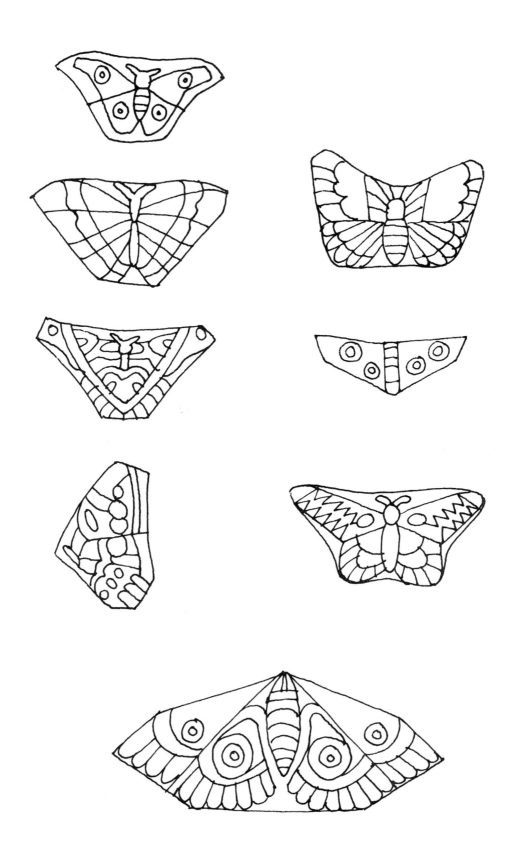

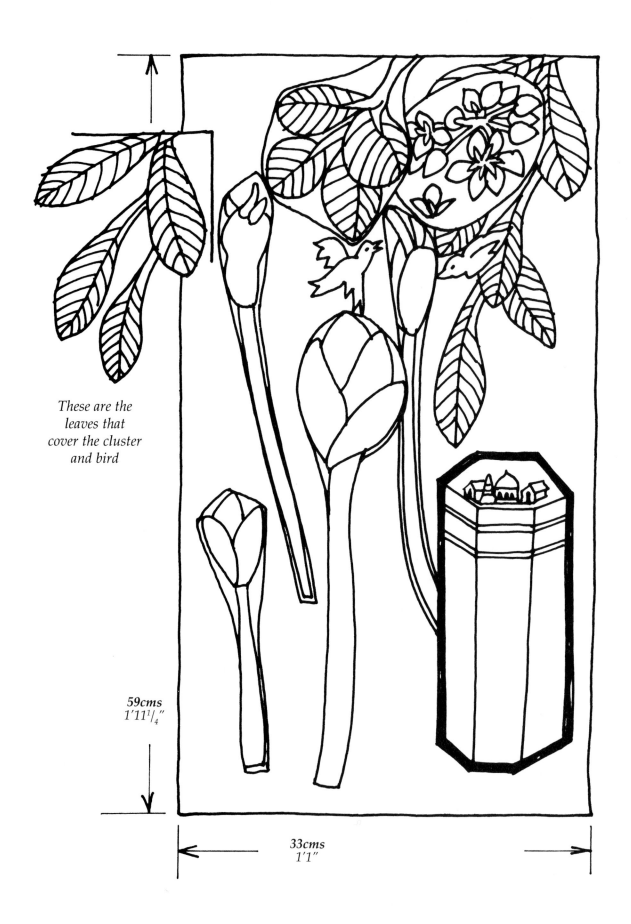

*These are the
leaves that
cover the cluster
and bird*

59cms
1'11¹/₄"

33cms
1'1"

59cms
1'11¼"

56cms
1'10"

59cms
1'11¹/₄"

33cms
1'1"

58.5cms
1'11"

33.5cms
1'1¼"

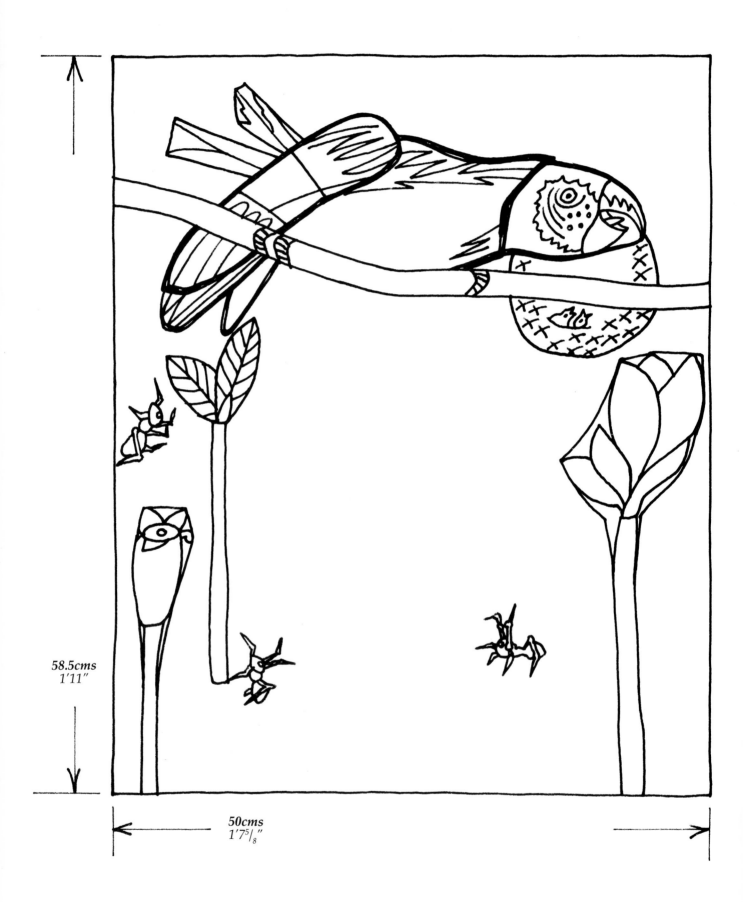

58.5cms
1'11"

50cms
1'7⁵/₈"

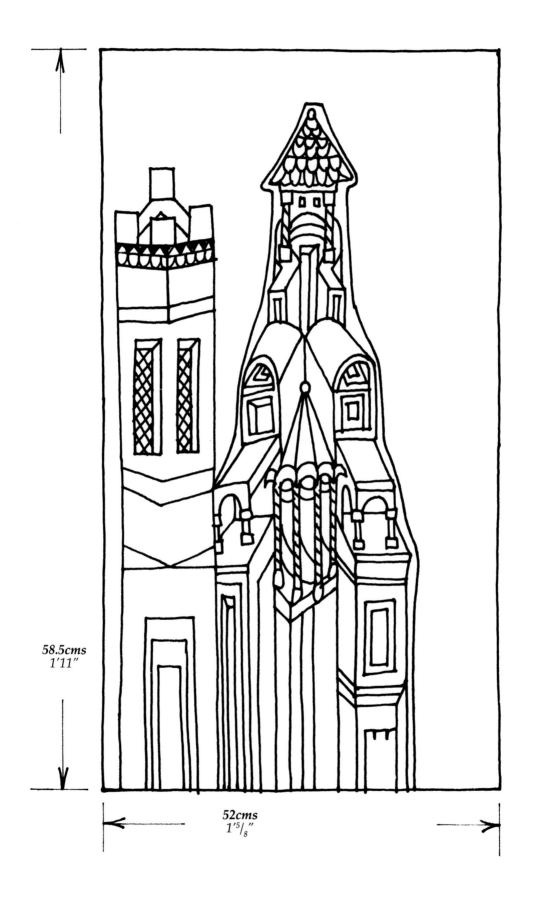

58.5cms
1'11"

52cms
1'5/8"

14cms
5$^{1}/_{2}$"

166cms
5'5$^{3}/_{8}$"

153cms
5'1$^{1}/_{4}$"

HOMESTEAD
QUILT

It is strange how memories can divert you from your original intention, which in this case was to design a repetitive house quilt using one of those little old houses found in country towns. Many years ago we lived in a mining town in a similar cottage to this. Apart from the plumbing, I had to cope with solitude, three young children and a wood stove. The stove proved to be my greatest comfort—after I discovered the secret of never letting it go out. I was terrified to go outside the picket fence with the children in case they wandered off and fell down an old mine shaft. In the early evening these were the colours that softened the bleak landscape beyond the picket fence.

INSTRUCTIONS
Size approx. 1.7m (5ft 6in) x 1.5m (5ft)

MATERIALS
5.5m (6yd) black cotton fabric for front and back
180cm (2yd) dark green cotton fabric
90cm (1yd) fabric each for the colours of the templates
180cm (2yd) dark blue cotton fabric
140cm (1$^1/_2$yd) black and white fabric
180cm (2yd) light grey and 180cm (2yd) khaki cotton
    fabric; these can also be used in the leaf borders
scrap-bag pieces for the leaves and the cottage

HOMESTEAD
QUILT

DIRECTIONS

Tear the dark blue cotton fabric into four pieces 40cm (16in) long by 36cm (14in) wide. Use the reverse of the black and white fabric for the tree trunks and Mallee fowl mound. Don't forget to draw the eggs in any white patches before you tint the mound. See illustration.

Always remember, when you trace the pattern pieces onto the material, to cut them out with a seam allowance. Turn this under and sew down with black thread and neaten edge with indelible marker. Assemble pieces and then appliqué onto the blue fabric. These images are very simple.

BEES, BABY BIRD, BLUE-TONGUED LIZARD AND EGG SHELL

Enlarge the patterns. These images can be traced straight onto the fine, green lawn fabric, by putting it over the inked drawing. Otherwise use carbon paper. Cut with a seam allowance around the edge, turn under and sew down etc. The same technique applies to the egg and the lizard, although the latter could be cut from a patterned material.

Before they are sewn in place the lizard is placed behind one tree branch and slightly over the top of another.

THE LITTLE HOUSE

Follow the illustrated pattern for this. It is straight piece-work. Try to find a material which gives the illusion of corrugated iron for the roof. If you use fine shirt cotton for the verandah posts the texture will give the authentic lopped tree-effect. These little houses were cosy, but hand built and so often were not symmetrical. In a repetitive design the dividing panels should be the small gum-leaf borders.

THE GUM LEAVES

Start by sewing two gum leaves together, then cut a curve into the blue and add them to that. The idea is to keep adding gum-leaf shapes with an occasional flash of blue or branch colour. Remember to keep working downwards on a 15cm (6in) width. Gum leaves hang straight down, or come in at an angle from the right or left hand side. This means you can have a clump of leaves dissecting another group, by once again cutting a curve across. This is not wasteful because if you have cut away a large piece, add this at another angle somewhere else. The idea is to try to achieve all this by piece-work. It is possible but I cheated with appliquéd leaves and branches when things got out of control. In the end this is impossible to pick, because when the border is finished and the side straightened with black and green strips, it is quilted. The veins of the leaves are drawn. These sides are attached to the finished centre. This top is then placed on the wadding and backing, pinned firmly, and quilted.

TEMPLATES (SAWTOOTH PATTERN)

See illustration. This is a well-known pattern. I love the combination of appliqué and traditional templates. It's a case of enjoying the best of both worlds.

TEMPLATES

The geometric shapes of traditional patchwork quilts are daunting to timid beginners or mathematically dyslectic admirers like myself. Fifteen years ago in Greece, my daughter Sally and I completed two quilts in six weeks. They were labours of love but appallingly inaccurate. Sal traced the templates and I cobbled them together. From this experience I evolved and patented a system which eliminates inaccuracy, frayed edges and distortion. The shapes, with a cutting and sewing line are printed onto non-woven fusible material. Top Templates for Quilt Tops, my easy foolproof method of assembly will be available soon. ◪

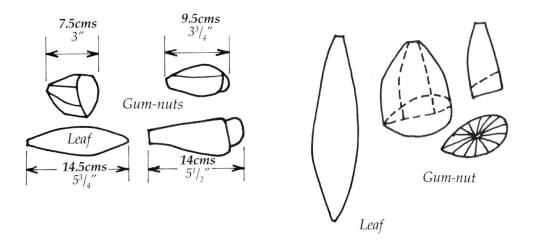

7.5cms 3"

9.5cms 3³/₄"

Gum-nuts

Leaf

14.5cms 5³/₄"

14cms 5¹/₂"

Leaf

Gum-nut

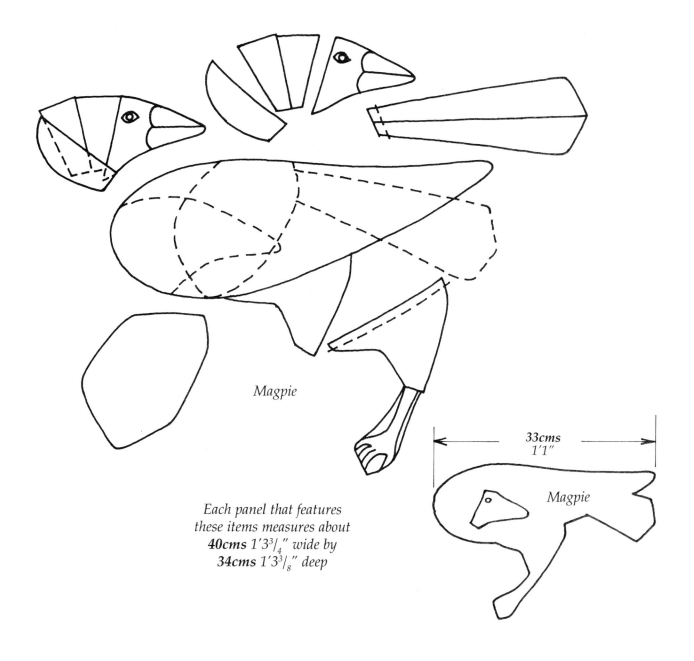

Magpie

*Each panel that features
these items measures about
40cms 1'3³/₄" wide by
34cms 1'3³/₈" deep*

33cms 1'1"

Magpie

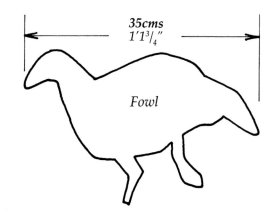

35cms
1'1³/₄"

Fowl

*Each panel that features
these items measures about
40cms 1'3³/₄" wide by
34cms 1'3³/₈" deep*

Fowl and nest

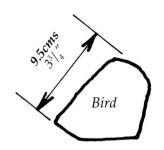

9.5cms
3³/₄"

Bird

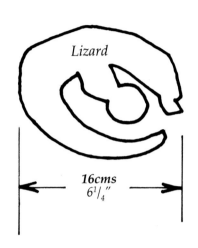

Lizard

16cms
6¹/₄"

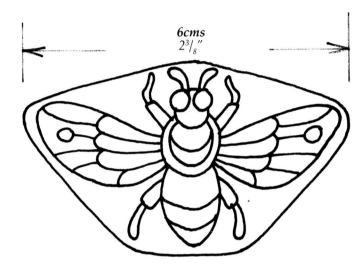

6cms
2³/₈"

Bee

Bird

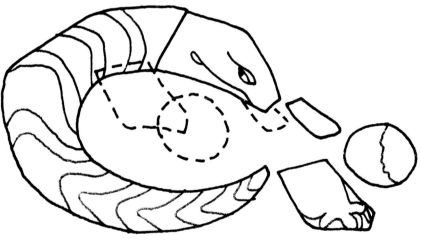

Lizard with egg

*Each panel that features
these items measures about
40cms 1'3³/₄" wide by
34cms 1'3³/₈" deep*

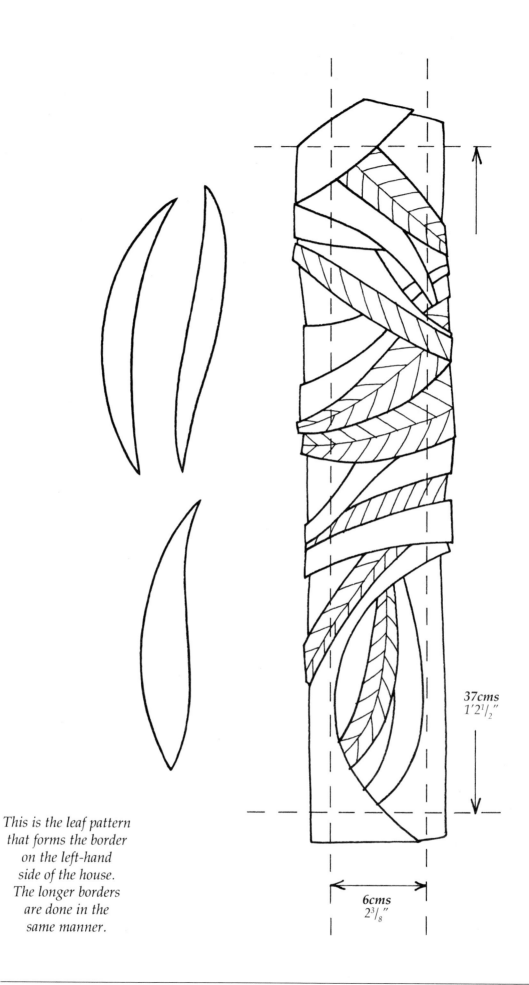

This is the leaf pattern that forms the border on the left-hand side of the house. The longer borders are done in the same manner.

37cms
$1'2^{1}/_{2}''$

6cms
$2^{3}/_{8}''$

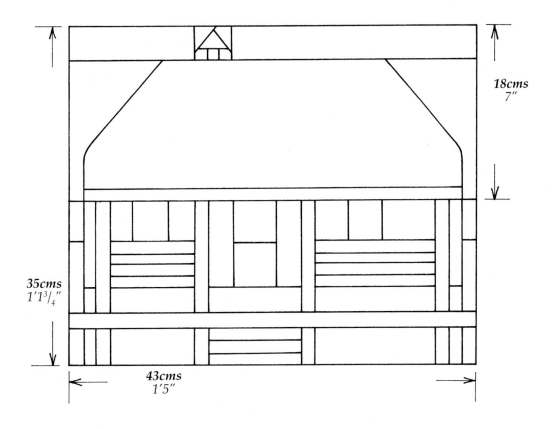

18cms
7"

35cms
1'1³/₄"

43cms
1'5"

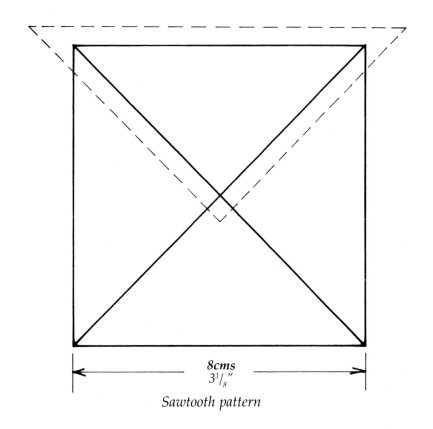

8cms
3¹/₈"

Sawtooth pattern

COWBOY
QUILT

The idea for this quilt came partly from my childhood. My first memory of a doll was an Indian squaw, and my first shoes, baby moccasins. Both came from an American Indian reservation, and were made of suede and fringed and beaded. I still have the moccasins with little worn patches on the pads.

At the age of four I was taken to Adelaide in South Australia to live with my cousin and her family. She became my mother, and her son, my brother. This is a memory for that brother, Robert, of our cowboy and Indian days when we fought each other through the wild and tangled garden of the old family home 'Highfield' at Glen Osmond in full regalia, with the ghost horses from the empty stables galloping across the sky.

COWBOY
QUILT

INSTRUCTIONS

Size approx. 1.7m (5ft 7in) square

Centre panel size approx 1.4m (4ft 7in) x 1.2m (4ft)

MATERIALS

5.5m (6yd) black cotton fabric for backing and border panels

3.6m (4yd) wadding

180cm (2yd) black polyester/cotton fabric for binding

90cm (1yd) striped fabric for vest, kerchief; use in reverse for kerchief

90cm (1yd) grey cotton fabric for pants

90cm (1yd) smoky fawn cotton fabric for larger horse

46cm (1/2yd) fabric each of suitable colours for the little horses

46cm (1/2yd) each of four different coloured abstract materials for the feathers; always use the reverse for this

90cm (1yd) shirt fabric

90cm (1yd) tan cotton fabric for border strip and halter

46cm (1/2yd) hat fabric; use a self-pattern that can be reversed

46cm (1/2yd) each of deep and light fawn fabric for the face and hands

Try to find suitable material for the gun, holster, buckles etc. in your scrap bag. This may also apply to the feathers and little horses. You may be able to find a fabric printed with stars for the background, or you could paint them yourself or just leave it plain.

DIRECTIONS

SMALL HORSES

The little horses are simple to follow from the illustrations. If possible use your own artists. My granddaughter was 5 when she drew my favourite six-legged pony.

THE LARGE HORSE

He is a very naïve nag. See illustration. Cut out the head shape with seam allowance. Assemble the left side of the face, put this behind the nose, turn under the seam allowance and sew down. Now bind the head except for the top. Appliqué the nostril in place, then the eye. Appliqué the mane in place, then attach the head to the neck etc. Draw mane with indelible marker. Sew halter in place.

THE HAT

Trace and cut out the three hat pieces. Bind in black. Hide seam with hat band. See illustration.

FACE

Study illustration carefully. Start with the eyes: 5cm x 8cm (2in x 3in) pieces of white cotton fabric. Attach the first piece to the outer corner of each eye and then the second along the bottom. Piece 3, black, goes across the other corners. Press and paint the eyes.

Trace and cut out the nose, lip, mouth and chin, with a seam allowance. Alternate the face colours. Place the nose over the lip section and cut a curve, sew and press. Place the mouth over the lip section, cut a curve, join together. Do the same with the bottom half of the mouth and the chin. Press. Join the left-hand side of the face to the middle section. Press. Pin the right-hand side to the face but before you sew, check to see if the eyes are level. Sew. Press and bind around the face in black. Bind the ear and the side of the neck. Pin in place and sew. Pin the hat over the top of the eyes and sew in place.

170cms
5'7"

137.25cms
4'6"

122cms
4'

172cms
5'7³/₄"

THE SHIRT AND SLEEVES

Cut a piece of shirt fabric 40cm (16in) long by 33cm (13in) wide. Sew a 5mm ($\frac{1}{4}$in) flap down the centre. Trace and cut out the sleeves and cuffs. Join the cuffs to the end of the sleeves and bind around both pieces.

VEST AND KERCHIEF

Cut the vest pieces and bind all around in black. Do the same for the two kerchief pieces. Sew the cowboy's face to the kerchief. The other piece goes behind the neck. Now assemble cowboy's body. See illustration. Sew down almost to belt.

PANTS

Cut out the legs. On the left leg sew a narrow line of black. See illustration. Bind the side of each leg. Pin the right leg slightly over the left and sew in place.

HANDS

These are very simple. Bind in black and mark fingers in running stitch. Pin to bottom of cuffs.

If you study the drawing of the cowboy, you will see the simple sequence of attaching his belts etc.

BELTS, HOLSTER ETC.

Trace and paint buckle designs and bind in black. The gun and holster are also bound in black. Do this separately for each piece and then sew down. The pants belt is bound in black. The gun belt is turned under, with a lighter piece sewn across the centre marker in 5mm ($\frac{1}{4}$in). See illustration.

Place one belt over the join of pants and body, and the gun belt across the body. Pin the holster behind the leg and the right hand, and the other hand behind the body. Sew all these down.

ASSEMBLY

First border the centre panel with black, then pin the cowboy and big horse into position and sew down. Pin the little horses in the sky and sew. The feathers are bound in black, and sewn to the side and top border strips. These borders are then attached to the centre with calico strips. A 5cm (2in) strip of tan fabric is added to the bottom. Quilt and back as usual. ⧓

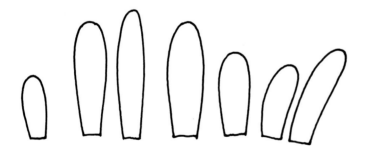

Select a number of basic shapes for the feathers or improvise your own, or use Winter Solstice feathers (p.55).

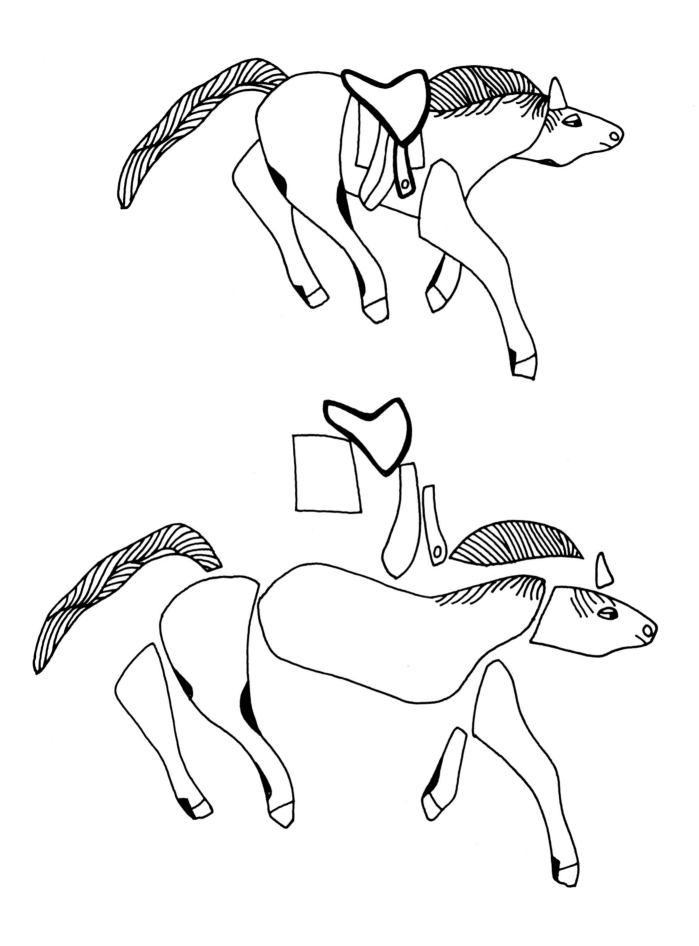

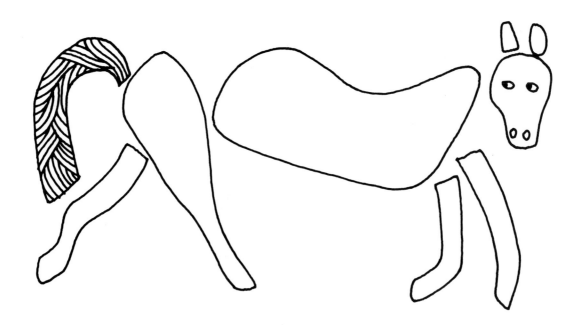

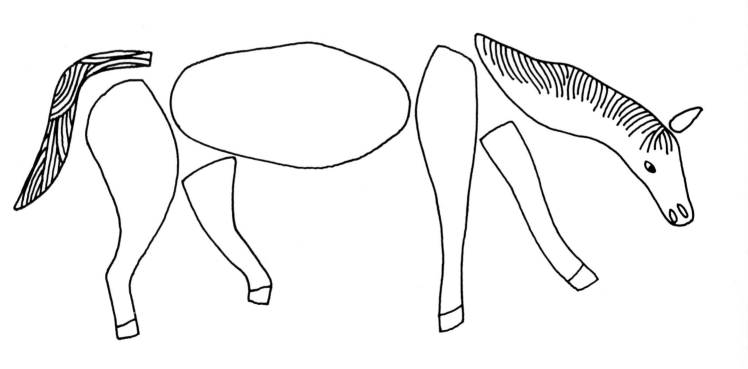

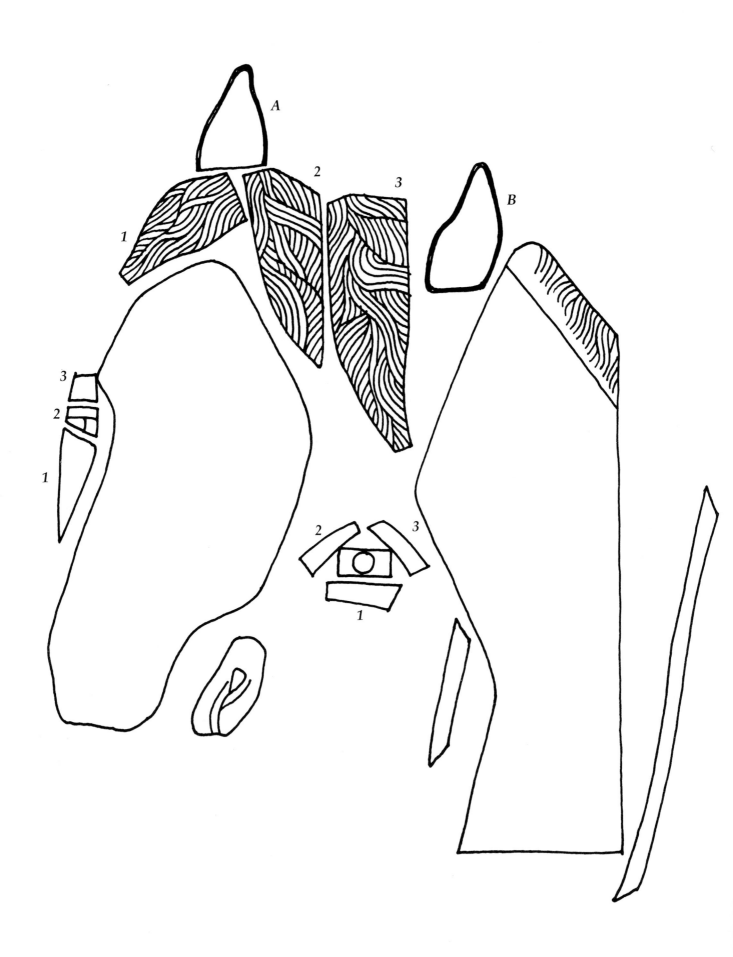

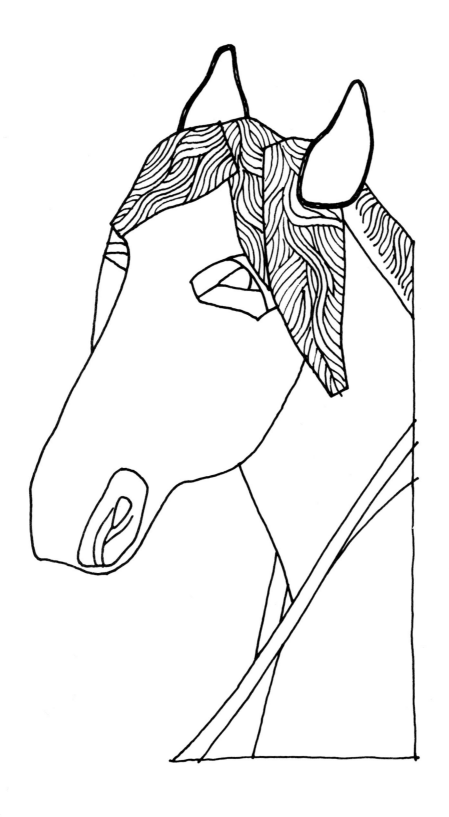

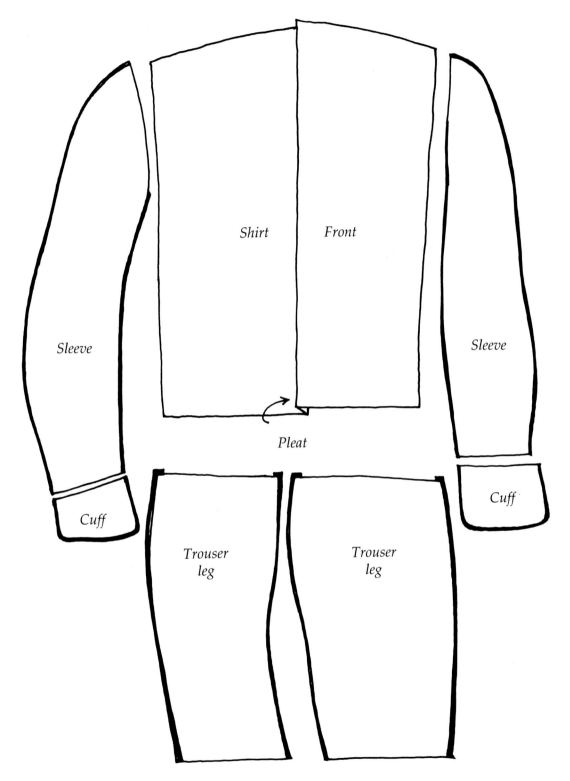

Underlying shapes of shirt and trousers

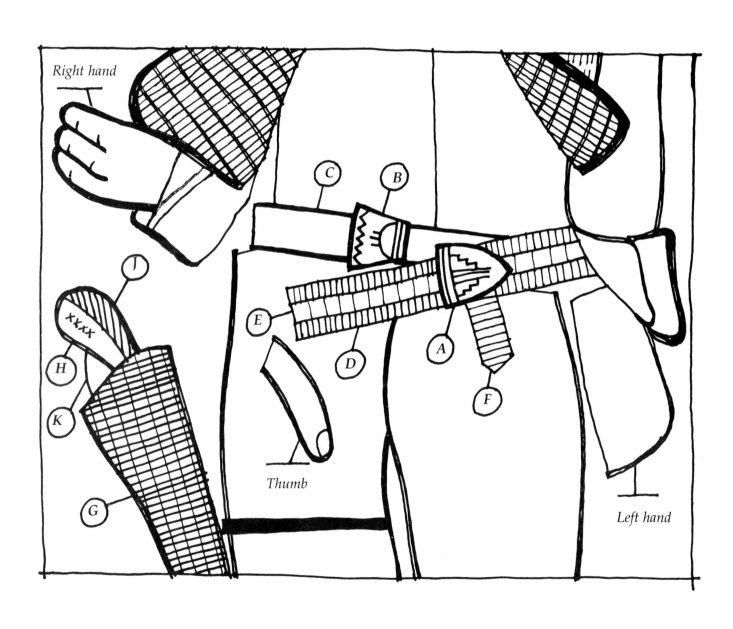

Right hand

Thumb

Left hand

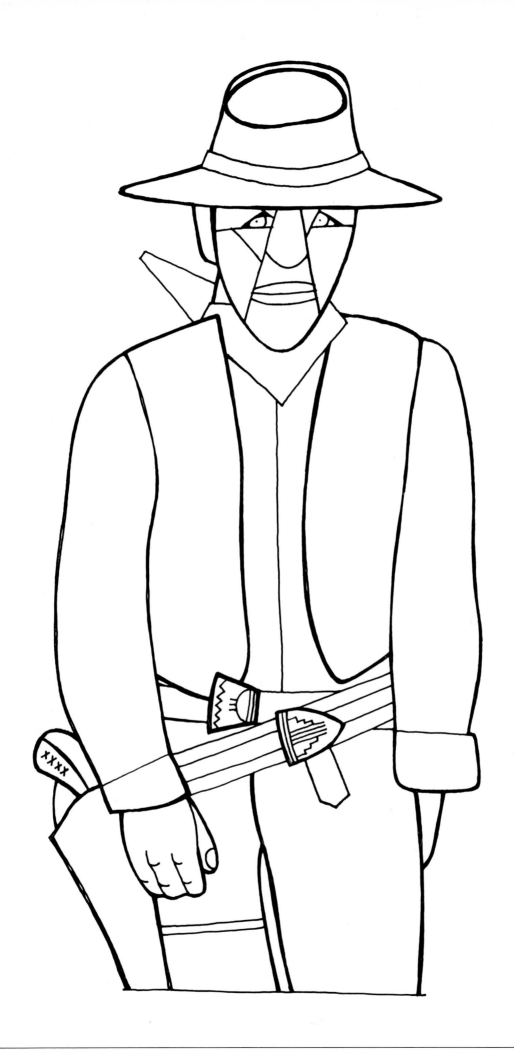

PRESIDENT'S

This is a tale of six mistakes; the first is obviously the biggest. About fifteen years ago my former young associate Lee McGorman and I took six months to appliqué a 6m (20ft) American flag wall-hanging featuring the Presidents' Wives from Martha Washington onwards. It was used as the backdrop for an official dinner for Nancy Kissinger at the Sydney Hilton. We were told to cover the stars with calico as a matter of protocol.

Second mistake, we agreed; but appliquéd an annoyed bald-headed eagle on the calico.

Nancy Kissinger was so impressed she thought Henry should buy the flag for the Nation and present it to the Smithsonian Institute.

Third mistake, she forgot to tell Henry.

Fourth mistake, in the intervening years we added another line to accommodate the new wives, Roslyn Carter and Nancy Reagan.

Fifth mistake, my son Matthew took it to New York and left it with our family lawyer. Unfortunately the lawyer went off his skull and it was lost for years.

Eventually it found its way to my daughter in San Diego and an Andy Warhol '15-minute brush with fame'. This took place on a showboat on San Diego harbour in 1988 at the opening of the Republican Womens' Presidential Campaign. Its final destination was supposed to be the Republican Rally in Washington and eventually the Smithsonian.

Sixth mistake. Sal's garage blew up and it was incinerated. But my old friend the bald-headed eagle survived and was sent back to Sydney to rise from the ashes like a phoenix as this new resolute President's quilt.

PRESIDENT'S

INSTRUCTIONS
Size approx. 1.6m (5ft 2in) square. This is difficult!
Centre panel approx. 1.3m (4ft 3in) x 1.1m (3ft 7in)

MATERIALS
5.5m (6yd) black cotton fabric for backing and borders
5.5m (4yd) wadding
180cm (2yd) calico
180cm (2yd) dark red cotton fabric
180cm (2yd) dark blue cotton fabric
180cm (2yd) fabric for main wing, 46cm ($^1/_2$yd) each for
    the two smaller wings—use tailor's remnants if
    possible; these give variations of colour
46cm ($^1/_2$yd) fabric for the tree trunk
46cm ($^1/_2$yd) fabric for the mountains
90cm (1yd) white satin, also used in reverse
46cm ($^1/_2$yd) cream brocade
additional feathers, beak and inside of the mouth from
    the scrap bag*

DIRECTIONS

THE EAGLE, IN OVERSEW
Use the grid to copy and enlarge the eagle, mountains
etc. to the correct size. See illustration.

Always keep the large drawing and position the
separate pieces on this so you place them in the right
position.

Trace the various sections from this cartoon.

Carefully study the illustration. Begin with Fig. 1.
Cut out the large wings A1 and A2.

Place these on the master drawing. Cut the next
feathers B1 and B2. They are placed on top of the large
wings. See illustration. The feathers C1 and C2 are
placed on top of B1 and B2. Finally cover the edges of
these pieces with the spine of the wing D1 and D2. Pin
all the pieces together, and finish in oversew. Press and
place back on the pattern. Use different shades of sewing
thread.

---

*This eagle is not for the faint hearted, he was done before I simplified my
technique.

156cms
5'1³/₈"

140cms
4'7"

105cms
3'5³/₈"

157cms
5'1³/₄"

THE BODY

The body and head shapes of the eagle are cut in one piece from the same fabric as the large wings. Cut chest feathers K. See illustration. Pin in place and sew with variegated threads, oversew. Pin claws and talons in place, and position this on the master drawing in front of the wings. Pin and then sew the wings to the body. Place back on the pattern. The idea is to have the bird completely sewn together before he is pinned to the background.

TAIL AND HEAD FEATHERS

Trace and cut out the main tail E. See illustration. Cut out the other feathers (see illustration) F1, F2, G1, G2 and H pin on top of tail shape. Mix the feather materials. Use unbleached sewing cotton (ecru), white is too obtrusive. Trace shape N (see illustration), top of head and neck feathers. Then shape O which goes under N. Pin and oversew these together. Oversew additional feathers P to the head N. Cut beak M1 and M2 and inside of mouth L. Pin the white head feathers over the brown body/head shape. Trim the back if necessary. Pin beak and tongue in place and oversew this to the head. Sew in the eye. Press and place this on the master drawing. Before you finish this section cut three extra feathers R1, R2, and R3 from the same material as the brown chest feathers. Pin these, two on the left and one on the right behind the main wings near the body.

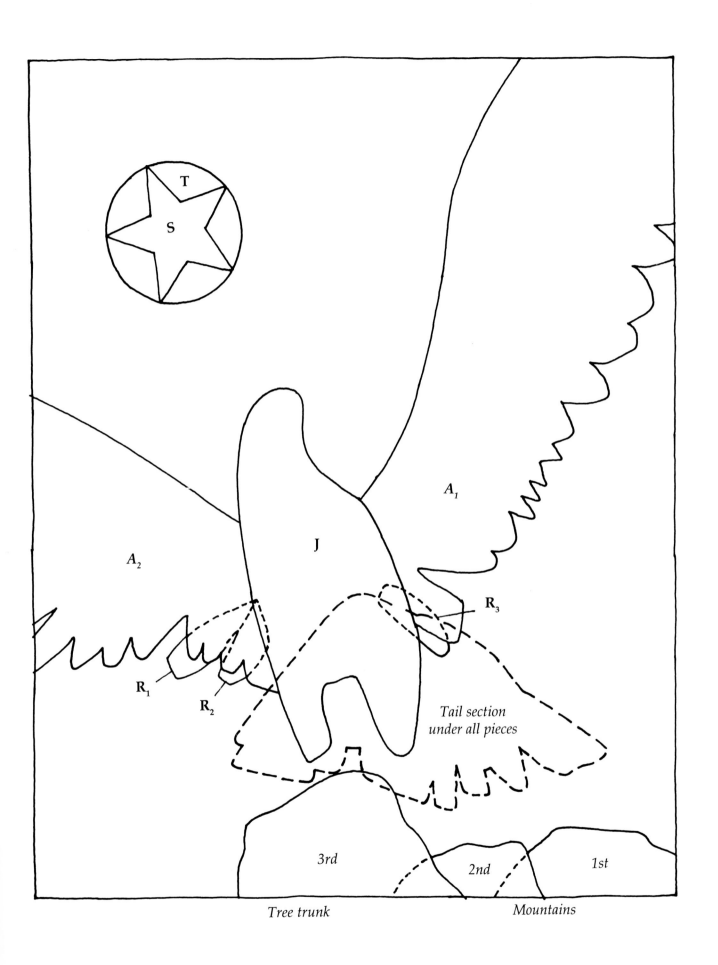

Tail section
under all pieces

3rd

2nd

1st

Tree trunk

Mountains

TREE TRUNK AND MOUNTAINS

Three simple pieces. Decorate the tree trunk with running stitch then pin it and the mountains along the bottom edge of the background. See illustration.

TEMPLATE STRIP BORDERS

Join 5cm (2in) strips of dark red and calico, make these 15cm (6in) longer than the centre panel. Press, cut in 5cm (2in) pieces and rejoin alternately. Border one side with dark red and the other with black. See illustration. Widen these borders. End with calico and dark blue. Join these two sides to the main piece. The top and bottom borders are black, calico, dark-red and blue. Put this finished top on the wadding and the backing 5cm (2in) wider all round. Pin these firmly. Then in a very simple outline, quilt the eagle. Use a loose tension and smooth carefully as you go. Sew down the black lines in the borders. Finally turn the backing over the front and finish off the edge. ◪

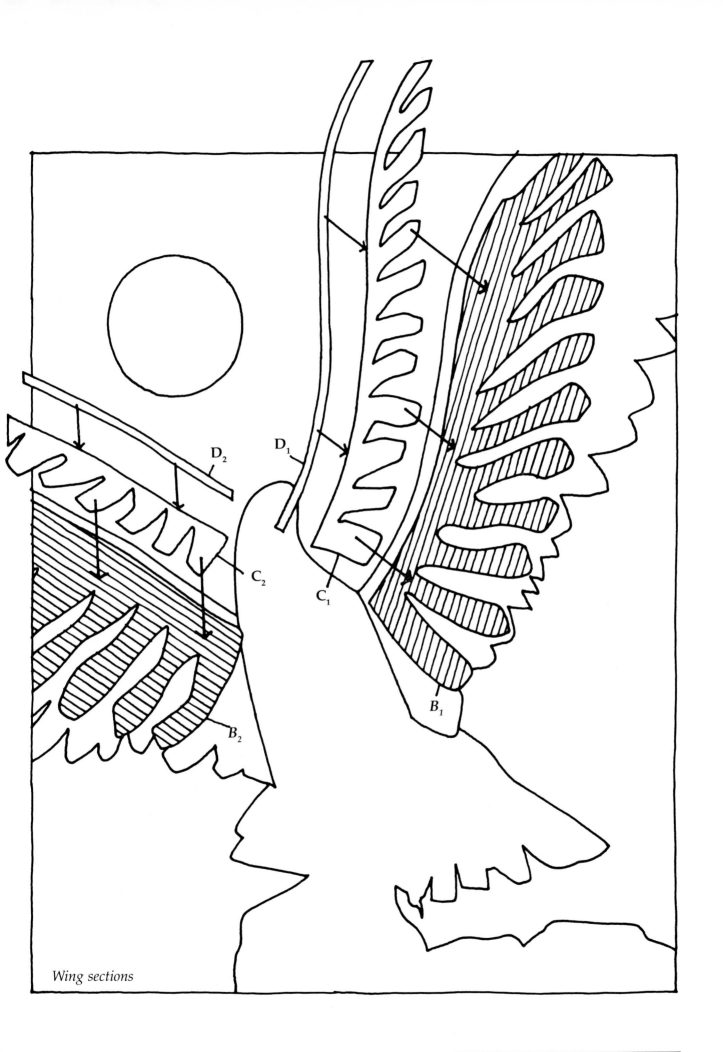

Wing sections

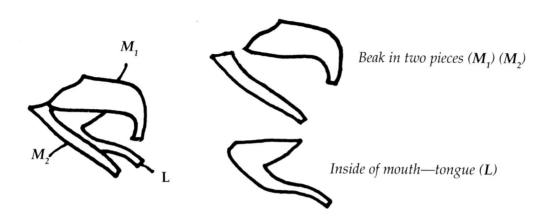

Beak in two pieces (M_1) (M_2)

*Inside of mouth—tongue (**L**)*

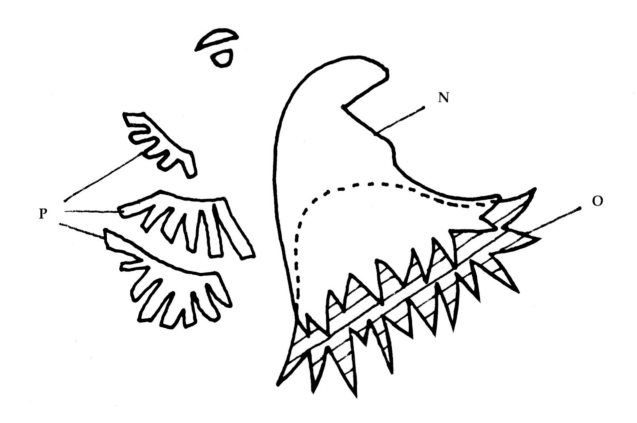

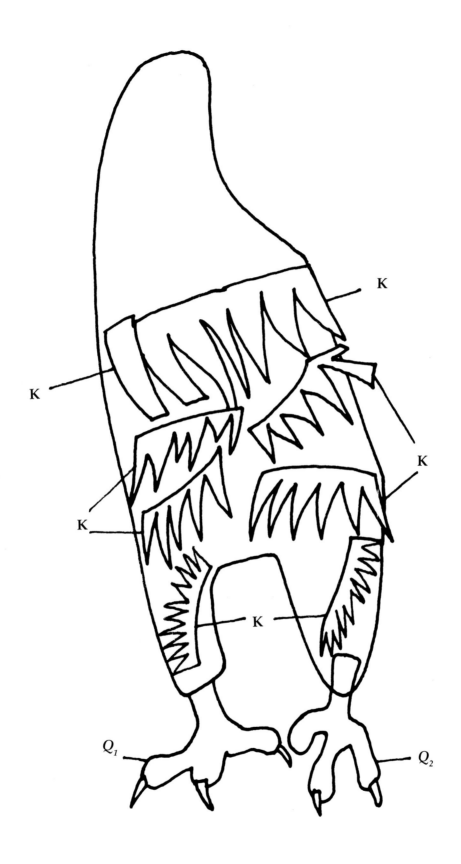

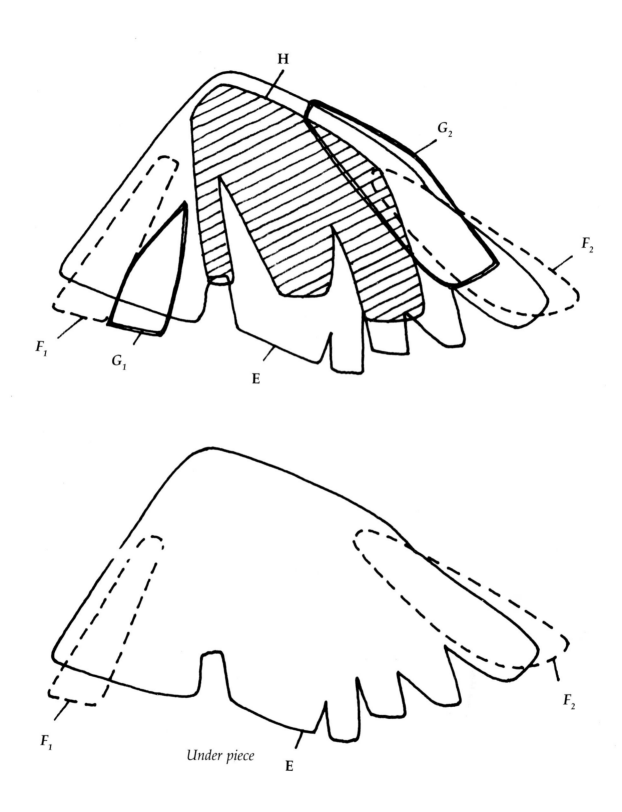

Under piece